THE FROZEN DEEP
and
MR WRAY'S CASH-BOX

WILKIE COLLINS

THE FROZEN DEEP
and
MR WRAY'S CASH-BOX

ALAN SUTTON PUBLISHING LIMITED

The Frozen Deep first published in 1874
Mr Wray's Cash-box first published in 1852

First published in this edition in the United Kingdom in 1996
Alan Sutton Publishing Limited
Phoenix Mill · Far Thrupp · Stroud · Gloucestershire · GL5 2BU

British Library Cataloguing in Publication Data

A catalogue record for this book is available from the British Library.

Cover picture: *detail from* Summer Evening at Skagen, the Artist's Wife with a Dog on the Beach, *1892 by Peder Severin Kroyer (1851–1909). (Skagens Museum, Denmark/Bridgeman Art Library, London.)*

Typeset in 9/10 Bembo.
Typesetting and origination by
Alan Sutton Publishing Limited.
Printed in Great Britain by
The Guernsey Press Company Limited,
Guernsey, Channel Islands.

CONTENTS

BIOGRAPHICAL INTRODUCTION

WILLIAM WILKIE COLLINS was born in Marylebone on 8 January 1824. He died sixty-five years later in Wimpole Street, little more than three blocks away, and lived most of his life in that central part of London. Yet from that narrow base he managed to live as colourful a life as any other Victorian and wrote some of the most gripping novels of the nineteenth century. He is still regarded as 'the father of the detective story' and 'the novelist who invented sensation'. He himself put it more modestly. He was, he said, just a simple story teller.

Such stories, however, included *The Moonstone* and *The Woman in White*. His first published novel, *Antonina*, appeared in 1851, and his last, *Blind Love*, had to be finished by an old friend, Walter Besant, in 1889. In the intervening years Collins wrote over thirty novels and collections of stories, as well as a biography of his father William Collins. The manuscript of the first novel he actually wrote, though it was turned down by every publisher he approached and vanished for nearly 150 years, finally surfaced in New York in 1990. Entitled *Iolani; Or Tahiti as it Was*, its somewhat belated publication is now planned. Collins himself was remarkably frank about that early failure. 'My youthful imagination ran riot among the noble savages, in scenes which caused the respectable British publisher [actually Chapman and Hall] to declare that it was impossible to put his name on the title page of such a novel.'

It was during the writing of that first, unsuccessful, novel that Collins' parents first became fully aware that all their assumptions about 'Willy's future' (as he was known in the family) were quite wrong. His father, William Collins, already an RA, with a string of wealthy clients, including the late George IV, was a leading landscape artist and had readily assumed that both sons (Charles Allston Collins was two years younger than Wilkie) would also take up painting. William's own father, another William, was a picture dealer and Harriet, Wilkie Collins's mother, came from a family of painters. Both Constable and Linnell were close friends of the family as the boys grew up in Hampstead, and sketching became second nature to them both.

Yet it was the written word and a good story well told that tugged at Wilkie Collins. He later described how at his second school at Highbury, where he was a boarder, he was regularly bullied at night by the head boy.

'You will go to sleep, Collins,' he was apparently told, 'when you have told me a story.' Quite an incentive. 'It was this brute who first awakened in me, his poor little victim, a power of which but for him I might never have been aware. . . . When I left school I continued story telling for my own pleasure.'

The occasions when he could do so were varied indeed. His school days were remarkably interrupted by his father's decision to take the family to Italy for two years, an extended visit that gave Collins not only visual stimuli but provided the background for what would be his first published novel, *Antonina*. It was also in Italy that, according to Dickens, Collins experienced his 'first love adventure'. As Dickens explained the affair to his sister-in-law later, it 'had proceeded, if I may be allowed the expression, to the utmost extremities'. Collins was thirteen at the time. Perhaps more important, for his writing if not his character, it was probably in Italy that his attraction to the visual began to seek an alternative outlet to painting, and where the embryo writer began to emerge from the family of artists.

When, a few years later, his father was considering whether Wilkie should be entered at art school, prior to applying to the Royal Academy, it was already clear that his interests lay elsewhere. One idea was that he should go to Oxford, before entering the Church. But William was eventually persuaded that a spell in a tea merchant's office would at least provide Wilkie with a more secure income than the desultory writing that seemed to attract him. It did not last, though since the office in the Strand was near all the publishers it at least allowed him to trail round them with his articles in spare moments. He had his first short story, *The Last Stage Coachman*, published under his name in *The Illuminated Magazine* at this time. His father's next initiative was to arrange for Wilkie to enter Lincoln's Inn and to read for the Bar, again on the assumption that it might provide a better source of income than writing. It was to be one of William's last family concerns, for he died the following year, in 1847.

Collins managed to sustain his legal studies, or at least his necessary attendances, sufficiently over the next few years to be finally called to the Bar in 1851. It may not have been a particularly attractive calling, in his eyes, but it was later to serve its purpose. Eight of his novels have lawyers as prominent characters and the drawing up of wills was crucial to several of his later plots, including *The Woman in White*. When his father died, Collins, though still ostensibly studying for the Bar, had reached the third chapter of the second volume of *Antonina*, and had already read the bulk of the first volume to his father. Thereafter he immediately laid the novel aside and took up the preparations for a memoir of his father. It was thus a biographical work, *The Life of William Collins*, and not a novel that in

1848 became his first published work and established his name in the publishing world.

With the death of William Collins his family, though saddened by his suffering, were soon showing a new kind of independence. His love for them had never been in doubt, but William had early acquired a streak of moral rectitude which over the years irritated his friends and restricted his family. Wilkie had probably felt the heavy hand more than his brother Charles, but had chosen to ride the storms when they occurred, while pursuing his personal inclinations as best he could. Once the memoirs were completed, Harriet and her two sons settled down in an imposing house overlooking Regents Park, where she was happy to play host to her sons' younger friends from the artistic and literary worlds. It was here that Wilkie came under the wing of Charles Dickens and his brother befriended John Millais, William Holman-Hunt and other Pre-Raphaelites.

It was in this period that Wilkie Collins extended the range of his writing, providing leading articles for *The Leader*, short stories and essays for *Bentley's Miscellany*, a travel book about Cornwall entitled *Rambles Beyond Railways*, as well as dramatic criticisms and a short play. Charles Dickens had already enticed him to participate in the private theatricals he was developing and within eighteen months Wilkie had performed, in a small part, at a Dickens-directed charity performance in the presence of Queen Victoria. It was a short step from this to a joint production of Wilkie's first play, *The Lighthouse*, and a later commercial production at the Olympic Theatre. Soon they were co-operating on Dickens's journal *Household Words* and, with Wilkie in the lead, nicely egged on by Dickens, sharing colourful entertainments and distractions together in London and Paris.

It was a time when Collins began to write the kind of novels that were always to be identified with him, combining well-constructed plots with strong characters, beginning with *Basil* in the early fifties, followed by *Hide and Seek, After Dark* (short stories) and *The Dead Secret*, and culminating in *The Woman in White* in 1860. It was also the time when he met the two women – Caroline Graves and Martha Rudd – who were to weave in and out of his life for the next thirty years.

Caroline Graves appeared first, dramatically if Collins himself is to be believed, in much the same way as the mysterious lady in St John's Wood at the outset of *The Woman in White*. The story goes that the woman in distress gave a piercing scream one moonlit night as Wilkie and his brother were accompanying John Millais back to his lodgings. Millais simply exclaimed 'What a lovely woman'. Wilkie followed her into the darkness and later told them that she was a lady of good birth who had fallen into the clutches of a man who was threatening her life.

An element of truth perhaps, but it was tinged with Collins's undoubted story-telling ability. We now know that Caroline came from a humble family in the west country, had been married young, had a child and had been left a widow. It was not long before Collins was sharing lodgings with her, even answering letters openly from the various addresses they occupied in and around Marylebone. He even put her down as his wife, quite inaccurately, in the Census of 1861. He shared his triumphs with her, from *The Woman in White* onwards, but in spite of her obvious wishes, he was determined not to marry her.

These were the years of Collins's best-known novels. *The Woman in White* was followed by *Armadale* (for which he received the, then record, sum of £5,000 before a word had been written), *No Name* and *The Moonstone*. It was the preparation of *Armadale* and the writing of *The Moonstone*, however, that were to produce such dramatic upheavals in his private life and, to some extent, account for what many critics have detected as a relative falling off in his narrative power as a novelist.

His search for background for *Armadale* took him to the Norfolk Broads and to the small coastal village of Winterton. There, or nearby, he met Martha Rudd the nineteen-year-old daughter of a large, though poor, family. Her parents and relations have been traced (their graves are still in the local churchyard), but the timing of Martha's move to be closer to Collins in London remains obscure. What we do know is that only a few years later, when Collins was writing instalments of *The Moonstone*, already laid low by an acute attack of rheumatic gout and grieving over the death of his mother, Caroline decided to leave him and to marry a much younger man. Dickens felt that she had tried to bluff Collins into marriage and had failed. It could also have been Martha's appearance in London that proved to be the last straw.

Collins was devastated and finished *The Moonstone* in a haze of pain and with increasing doses of laudanum. It was a habit he was to follow for the rest of his life, his intake of opium eventually reaching remarkable levels, with inevitable repercussions on his writing ability. The domestic drama, however, was not yet over. Within nine months of Caroline's marriage, Martha, living in lodgings in Bolsover Street, was to bear Collins his first child and within another two years Caroline had left her husband and returned to Collins in Gloucester Place and Martha was pregnant with his second child.

And so it continued for the rest of his life, with Caroline once more established in Gloucester Place, though probably as housekeeper and hostess rather than mistress, and Martha and his 'morganatic' family (eventually two girls and a boy: Marian, Harriet and William Charles) not far away. When he visited Martha he became William Dawson, Barrister-at-Law, and she was known as Mrs Dawson. His male friends readily accepted these arrangements, though their wives were rarely, if ever, invited to Gloucester Place or, later, Wimpole Street.

His two families, basically Caroline's grandchildren and Martha's children, happily mingled together on holiday in Ramsgate and even occasionally in Gloucester Place, but Martha and Caroline never met. It was against this domestic background, with a host of literary and theatrical friends, that he pursued the last decade and a half of his life, completing some of his more socially conscious novels, like *Poor Miss Finch*, *The Haunted Hotel*, *The New Magdalen*, *The Black Robe*, and *Jezebel's Daughter*.

He died in Wimpole Street in September 1889, and was buried at Kensal Green Cemetery. Caroline was eventually buried with him and Martha continued to tend the grave until she left London. She died in Southend in 1919. The gold locket Wilkie gave Martha in 1868, marking the death of his mother, is still in the possession of my wife, Faith, their great-granddaughter.

WILLIAM M. CLARKE

Further Reading

Ashley, R., *Wilkie Collins*, London, 1952.

Clarke, William M., *The Secret Life of Wilkie Collins*, Stroud, 1996.

Peters, Catherine, *The King of Inventors: A Life of Wilkie Collins*, London, 1991.

Robinson, Kenneth, *Wilkie Collins*, London, 1951 & 1974.

THE FROZEN DEEP

To

OLIVER WENDELL HOLMES

In sincere admiration of his genius as poet, novelist, essayist and in cordial remembrance of our intercourse during my visit to America

INTRODUCTORY LINES

(Relating the Adventures and Transformations of The Frozen Deep.*)*

As long ago as the year 1856 I wrote a play called 'The Frozen Deep.'

The work was first represented by amateur actors, at the house of the late Charles Dickens, on the 6 of January 1857. Mr Dickens himself played the principal part, and played it with a truth, vigour, and pathos never to be forgotten by those who were fortunate enough to witness the performance. The other personages of the story were represented by the ladies of Mr Dickens's family, by the late Mark Lemon (editor of 'Punch'), by the late Augustus Egg, R.A. (the artist), and by the author of the play.

The next appearance of 'The Frozen Deep' (played by the amateur company) took place at The Gallery of Illustration, Regent Street, before the Queen and the Royal Family, by the Queen's own command. After this special performance other representations of the work were given – first at The Gallery of Illustration, subsequently (with professional actresses) in some of the principal towns in England – for the benefit of the family of a well-beloved friend of ours, who died in 1857 – the late Douglas Jerrold. At Manchester the play was twice performed – on the second evening in the presence of three thousand spectators. This was, I think, the finest of all the representations of 'The Frozen Deep.' The extraordinary intelligence and enthusiasm of the great audience stimulated us all to do out best. Dickens surpassed himself. The trite phrase is the true phrase to describe that magnificent piece of acting. He literally electrified the audience.

I present here, as 'a curiosity' which may be welcome to some of my readers, a portion of the original playbill of the performance at Manchester. To me it has now become one of the saddest memorials of the past that I possess. Of the nine amateur actors who played the men's parts (one of them my brother, all of them my valued friends) but two are now living besides myself – Mr Charles Dickens, jun., and Mr Edward Pigott.

The country performances being concluded, nearly ten years passed before the footlights shone again on 'The Frozen Deep.' In 1866 I accepted a proposal, made to me by Mr Horace Wigan, to produce the

In Remembrance of the late Mr Douglas Jerrold

FREE TRADE HALL
UNDER THE MANAGEMENT OF MR CHARLES DICKENS
On FRIDAY Evening, Aug. 21, and on SATURDAY
Evening, Aug. 22, 1857,

AT EIGHT O'CLOCK EXACTLY,

Will be presented an entirely new Romantic Drama, in three Acts, by

MR WILKIE COLLINS,
CALLED
THE FROZEN DEEP.

The Overture composed expressly for this Piece by Mr FRANCESCO BERGER,
who will conduct the Orchestra.

The Dresses by MESSRS NATHAN, *of Titchbourne Street, Haymarket, and* MISS WILKINS,
of Carburton St., Fitzroy Square. Perruquier, MR WILSON, *of the Strand.*

CAPTAIN EBSWORTH (*of the 'Sea-Mew'*)	MR EDWARD PIGOTT
CAPTAIN HELDING (*of the 'Wanderer'*)	MR ALFRED DICKENS
LIEUTENANT CRAYFORD	MR MARK LEMON
FRANK ALDERSLEY	MR WILKIE COLLINS
RICHARD WARDOUR	MR CHARLES DICKENS
LIEUTENANT STEVENTON	MR YOUNG CHARLES*
JOHN WANT (*Ship's Cook*)	MR AUGUSTUS EGG
BATESON (*two of the 'Sea-Mew's' people*)	MR SHIRLEY BROOKS
DARKER	MR CHARLES COLLINS

(OFFICERS AND CREWS OF THE 'SEA-MEW' AND 'WANDERER.')

MRS STEVENTON	MRS GEORGE VINING
ROSE EBSWORTH	MISS ELLEN SABINE
LUCY CRAYFORD	MISS ELLEN TERNAN
CLARA BURNHAM	MISS MARIA TERNAN
NURSE ESTHER	MRS TERNAN
MAID	MISS MEWTE†

The Scenery and Scenic Effects of the First Act by Mr TELBIN.
The Scenery and Scenic Effects of the Second and Third Acts by Mr STANFIELD, R.A.

★ A facetious nickname, invented by Charles Dickens for his eldest son.
† Another nickname by Dickens for a young lady who had nothing to say.

play (with certain alterations and additions) on the public stage, at the Olympic Theatre, London. The first performance took place (while I was myself absent from England) on the 27th of November, in the year just mentioned. Mr H. Neville acted the part 'created' by Dickens.

Seven years passed after the production of the play at the Olympic Theatre, and then 'The Frozen Deep' appealed once more to public favour, in another country than England, and under a totally new form.

I occupied the autumn and winter of 1873–74 most agreeably to myself, by a tour in the United States of America, receiving from the generous people of that great country a reception which I shall remember proudly and gratefully to the end of my life. During my stay in America I read in public, in the principal cities, one of my shorter stories (enlarged and re-written for the purpose), called 'The Dream-Woman.' Concluding my tour at Boston, I was advised by my friends to give, if possible, a special attraction to my farewell reading in America, by presenting to my audience a new work. Having this object in view, and having but a short space of time at my disposal, I bethought myself of 'The Frozen Deep.' The play had never been published, and I determined to re-write it in narrative form for a public reading. The experiment proved, on trial, to be far more successful than I had ventured to anticipate. Occupying nearly two hours in its delivery, the transformed 'Frozen Deep' kept its hold from first to last on the interest and sympathies of the audience. I hope to have future opportunities of reading it in my own country, as well as in the United States.

Proposals having lately been made to me, in England and in America, to publish my 'readings,' I here present 'The Frozen Deep'. The story, as I print it, is considerably longer than the story as I read it, the limits of time in the case of a public reading rendering it imperatively necessary to abridge without mercy developments of character and incident which are essential to the due presentation of a work in its literary form. I have only to add, for the benefit of those who may have seen, and who may not have forgotten, the play, that the narrative version of 'The Frozen Deep' departs widely from the treatment of the story in the First Act of the dramatic version, but (with the one exception of the Third Scene) follows the play as closely as possible in the succeeding Acts.

W.C.

LONDON:
September, 1874.

FIRST SCENE

THE BALL-ROOM

CHAPTER I

The date is between twenty and thirty years ago. The place is an English sea-port. The time is night. And the business of the moment is – dancing.

The Mayor and Corporation of the town are giving a grand ball, in celebration of the departure of an Arctic expedition from their port. The ships of the expedition are two in number – the *Wanderer* and the *Sea-Mew*. They are to sail (in search of the North-West Passage) on the next day, with the morning tide.

Honour to the Mayor and Corporation! It is a brilliant ball. The band is complete. The room is spacious. The large conservatory opening out of it is pleasantly lit with Chinese lantens and beautifully decorated with shrubs and flowers. All officers of the army and navy who are present wear their uniforms in honour of the occasion. Among the ladies the display of dresses (a subject which men don't understand) is bewildering, and the average of beauty (a subject which the men do understand) is the highest average attainable in all parts of the room.

For the moment the dance which is in progress is a quadrille. General admiration selects two of the ladies who are dancing as its favourite objects. One is a dark beauty in the prime of womanhood – the wife of First Lieutenant Crayford, of the *Wanderer*. The other is a young girl, pale and delicate, dressed simply in white, with no ornament on her head, but her own lovely brown hair. This is Miss Clara Burnham – an orphan. She is Mrs Crayford's dearest friend, and she is to stay with Mrs Crayford during the Lieutenant's absence in the Arctic regions. She is now dancing, with the Lieutenant himself for partner, and with Mrs Crayford and Captain Helding (Commanding Officer of the *Wanderer*) for *vis-à-vis* – in plain English, for opposite couple.

The conversation between Captain Helding and Mrs Crayford, in one of the intervals of the dance, turns on Miss Burnham. The captain is greatly interested in Clara. He admires her beauty, but he thinks her manner, for a young girl, strangely serious and subdued. Is she in delicate health?

Mrs Crayford shakes her head, sighs mysteriously, and answers – 'In
very delicate health, Captain Helding.'

'Consumptive?'

'Not in the least.'

'I am glad to hear that. She is a charming creature, Mrs Crayford. She
interests me indescribably. If I was only twenty years younger – perhaps
(as I am not twenty years younger) I had better not finish the sentence? Is
it indiscreet, my dear lady, to inquire what is the matter with her?'

'It might be indiscreet on the part of a stranger,' said Mrs Crayford. 'An
old friend like you may make any inquiries. I wish I could tell you what
is the matter with Clara. It is a mystery to the doctors themselves. Some
of the mischief is due, in my humble opinion, to the manner in which
she has been brought up.'

'Aye! aye! A bad school, I suppose?'

'Very bad, Captain Helding. But not the sort of school which you have
in your mind at this moment. Clara's early years were spent in a lonely
old house in the Highlands of Scotland. The ignorant people about her
were the people who did the mischief which I have just been speaking
of. They filled her mind with the superstitions which are still respected as
truths in the wild north – especially the superstition called the Second
Sight.'

'God bless me!' cried the Captain, 'you don't mean to say she believes
in such stuff as that? In these enlightened times, too!'

Mrs Crayford looked at her partner with a satirical smile.

'In these enlightened times, Captain Helding, we only believe in
dancing tables, and in messages sent from the other world by spirits who
can't spell! By comparison with such superstitions as these, even the
Second Sight has something – in the shape of poetry – to recommend it,
surely? Estimate for yourself,' she continued seriously, 'the effect of such
surroundings as I have described on a delicate sensitive young creature – a
girl with a naturally imaginative temperament, leading a lonely neglected
life. Is it so very surprising that she should catch the infection of the
superstition about her? And is it quite incomprehensible that her nervous
system should suffer accordingly at a very critical period of her life?'

'Not at all, Mrs Crayford – not at all, ma'am, as you put it. Still it is a
little startling, to a commonplace man like me, to meet a young lady at a
ball who believes in the Second Sight. Does she really profess to see into
the future? Am I to understand that she positively falls into a trance, and
sees people in distant countries, and foretells events to come? That is the
Second Sight, is it not?'

'That is the Second Sight, Captain. And that is, really and positively,
what she does.'

'The young lady who is dancing opposite to us?'

'The young lady who is dancing opposite to us.'

The captain waited a little – letting the new flood of information which had poured in on him settle itself steadily in his mind. This process accomplished, the Arctic explorer proceeded resolutely on his way to further discoveries.

'May I ask, ma'am, if you have ever seen her in a state of trance with your own eyes?' he inquired.

'My sister and I both saw her in the trance, little more than a month since,' Mrs Crayford replied. 'She had been nervous and irritable all the morning, and we took her out into the garden to breathe the fresh air. Suddenly, without any reason for it, the colour left her face. She stood between us, insensible to touch, insensible to sound, motionless as stone, and cold as death, in a moment. The first change we noticed came after a lapse of some minutes. Her hands began to move slowly, as if she was groping in the dark. Words dropped one by one from her lips, in a lost, vacant tone, as if she was talking in her sleep. Whether what she said referred to past or future I cannot tell you. She spoke of persons in a foreign country – perfect strangers to my sister and me. After a little interval, she suddenly became silent. A momentary colour appeared in her face, and left it again. Her eyes closed, her feet failed her, and she sank insensible into our arms.'

'Sank insensible into your arms,' repeated the captain, absorbing his new information. 'Most extraordinary! And – in this state of health – she goes out to parties, and dances. More extraordinary still!'

'You are entirely mistaken,' said Mrs Crayford. 'She is only here to-night to please me. And she is only dancing to please my husband. As a rule, she shuns all society. The doctor recommends change and amusement for her. She won't listen to him. Except on rare occasions like this, she persists in remaining at home.'

Captain Helding brightened at the allusion to the doctor. Something practical might be got out of the doctor. Scientific man. Sure to see this very obscure subject under a new light. 'How does it strike the doctor now?' said the captain. 'Viewed simply as a case, ma'am, how does it strike the doctor?'

'He will give no positive opinion,' Mrs Crayford answered. 'He told me that such cases as Clara's were by no means unfamiliar to medical practice. "We know," he told me, "that certain disordered conditions of the brain and the nervous system produce results quite as extraordinary as any that you have described – and there our knowledge ends. Neither my science, nor any man's science, can clear up the mystery in this case. It is an especially difficult case to deal with, because Miss Burnham's early associations dispose her to attach a superstitious importance to the malady – the hysterical malady, as some doctors would call it – from which she suffers. I can give you instructions for preserving her general health; and I can recommend you to try some change in her life – provided you first relieve her mind of any secret anxieties that may possibly be preying on it.'"

The captain smiled self-approvingly. The doctor had justified his anticipations. The doctor had suggested a practical solution of the difficulty.

'Aye! aye! At last we have hit the nail on the head! Secret anxieties. Yes! yes! Plain enough now. A disappointment in love – eh, Mrs Crayford?'

'I don't know, Captain Helding; I am quite in the dark. Clara's confidence in me – in other matters unbounded – is, in this matter of her (supposed) anxieties, a confidence still withheld. In all else we are like sisters. I sometimes fear there may indeed be some trouble preying secretly on her mind. I sometimes feel a little hurt at her incomprehensible silence.'

Captain Helding was ready with his own practical remedy for this difficulty.

'Encouragement is all she wants, ma'am. Take my word for it, this matter rests entirely with you. It's all in a nutshell. Encourage her to confide in you – and she *will* confide.'

'I am waiting to encourage her, Captain, until she is left alone with me – after you have all sailed for the Arctic Seas. In the meantime, will you consider what I have said to you as intended for your ear only? And will you forgive me if I own that the turn the subject has taken does not tempt me to pursue it any farther?'

The captain took the hint. He instantly changed the subject; choosing, on this occasion, safe professional topics. He spoke of ships that were ordered on foreign service; and, finding that these as subjects failed to interest Mrs Crayford, he spoke next of ships that were ordered home again. This last experiment produced its effect – an effect which the Captain had not bargained for.

'Do you know,' he began, 'that the *Atalanta* is expected back from the West Coast of Africa every day? Have you any acquaintances among the officers of that ship?'

As it so happened, he put those questions to Mrs Crayford while they were engaged in one of the figures of the dance which brought them within hearing of the opposite couple. At the same moment – to the astonishment of her friends and admirers – Miss Clara Burnham threw the quadrille into confusion by making a mistake! Everybody waited to see her set the mistake right. She made no attempt to set it right – she turned deadly pale, and caught her partner by the arm.

'The heat!' she said faintly. 'Take me away – take me into the air!'

Lieutenant Crayford instantly led her out of the dance, and took her into the cool and empty conservatory at the end of the room. As a matter of course, Captain Helding and Mrs Crayford left the quadrille at the same time. The captain saw his way to a joke.

'Is this the trance coming on?' he whispered. 'If it is, as commander of the Arctic Expedition, I have a particular request to make. Will the Second Sight oblige me by seeing the shortest way to the North-West Passage before we leave England?'

Mrs Crayford declined to humour the joke. 'If you will excuse my leaving you,' she said quietly, 'I will try and find out what is the matter with Miss Burnham.'

At the entrance to the conservatory Mrs Crayford encountered her husband. The Lieutenant was of middle age, tall and comely; a man with a winning simplicity and gentleness in his manner, and an irresistible kindness in his brave blue eyes. In one word, a man whom everybody loved – including his wife.

'Don't be alarmed,' said the Lieutenant. 'The heat has overcome her – that's all.'

Mrs Crayford shook her head, and looked at her husband, half satirically, half fondly.

'You dear old Innocent!' she exclaimed, 'that excuse may do for *you*. For my part, I don't believe a word of it. Go and get another partner, and leave Clara to me.'

She entered the conservatory and seated herself by Clara's side.

CHAPTER II

'Now, my dear!' (Mrs Crayford began) 'what does this mean?'

'Nothing.'

'That won't do, Clara. Try again.'

'The heat of the room——'

'That won't do either. Say that you choose to keep your own secrets, and I shall understand what you mean.'

Clara's sad, clear grey eyes looked up for the first time in Mrs Crayford's face, and suddenly became dimmed with tears.

'If I only dared tell you!' she murmured. 'I hold so to your good opinion of me, Lucy – and I am so afraid of losing it.'

Mrs Crayford's manner changed. Her eyes rested gravely and anxiously on Clara's face.

'You know as well as I do that nothing can shake my affection for you,' she said. 'Do justice, my child, to your old friend. There is nobody here to listen to what we say. Open your heart, Clara. I see you are in trouble, and I want to comfort you.'

Clara began to yield. In other words, she began to make conditions.

'Will you promise to keep what I tell you a secret from every living creature?' she began.

Mrs Crayford met that question by putting a question on her side.

'Does "every living creature" include my husband?'

'Your husband more than anybody! I love him, I revere him. He is so noble; he is so good! If I told him what I am going to tell you, he would despise me. Own it plainly, Lucy, if I am asking too much in asking you to keep a secret from your husband.'

'Nonsense, child! When you are married you will know that the easiest of all secrets to keep is a secret from your husband. I give you my promise. Now begin!'

Clara hesitated painfully.

'I don't know how to begin!' she exclaimed with a burst of despair. 'The words won't come to me.'

'Then I must help you. Do you feel ill to-night? Do you feel as you felt that day when you were with my sister and me in the garden?'

'Oh, no.'

'You are not ill, you are not really affected by the heat – and yet you turn as pale as ashes, and you are obliged to leave the quadrille! There must be some reason for this.'

'There *is* a reason. Captain Helding——'

'Captain Helding! What in the name of wonder has the Captain to do with it?'

'He told you something about the *Atalanta*. He said the *Atalanta* was expected back from Africa immediately.'

'Well, and what of that? Is there anybody in whom you are interested coming home in the ship?'

'Somebody whom I am afraid of is coming home in the ship.'

Mrs Crayford's magnificent black eyes opened wide in amazement.

'My dear Clara! do you really mean what you say?'

'Wait a little, Lucy, and you shall judge for yourself. We must go back – if I am to make you understand me – to the year before we knew each other; to the last year of my father's life. Did I ever tell you that my father moved southward, for the sake of his health, to a house in Kent that was lent to him by a friend?'

'No, my dear. I don't remember ever hearing of the house in Kent. Tell me about it.'

'There is nothing to tell – except this. The new house was near a fine country seat standing in its own park. The owner of the place was a gentleman named Wardour. He, too, was one of my father's Kentish friends. He had an only son.'

She paused, and played nervously with her fan. Mrs Crayford looked at her attentively. Clara's eyes remained fixed on her fan – Clara said no more.

'What was the son's name?' asked Mrs Crayford, quietly.

'Richard.'

'Am I right, Clara, in suspecting that Mr Richard Wardour admired you?'

The question produced its intended effect. The question helped Clara to go on.

'I hardly knew at first,' she said, 'whether he admired me or not. He was very strange in his ways – headstrong, terribly headstrong and passionate; but generous and affectionate in spite of his faults of temper. Can you understand such a character?'

'Such characters exist by thousands. I have my faults of temper. I begin to like Richard already. Go on.'

'The days went by, Lucy, and the weeks went by. We were thrown very much together. I began, little by little, to have some suspicion of the truth.'

'And Richard helped to confirm your suspicions, of course?'

'No. He was not – unhappily for me – he was not that sort of man. He never spoke of the feeling with which he regarded me. It was I who saw it. I couldn't help seeing it. I did all I could to show that I was willing to be a sister to him, and that I could never be anything else. He did not understand me, or he would not – I can't say which.'

'"Would not" is the most likely, my dear. Go on.'

'It might have been as you say. There was a strange rough bashfulness about him. He confused and puzzled me. He never spoke out. He seemed to treat me as if our future lives had been provided for while we were children. What could I do, Lucy?'

'Do? You could have asked your father to end the difficulty for you.'

'Impossible! You forget what I have just told you. My father was suffering at that time under the illness which afterwards caused his death. He was quite unfit to interfere.'

'Was there no one else who could help you?'

'No one.'

'No lady in whom you could confide?'

'I had acquaintances among the ladies in the neighbourhood. I had no friends.'

'What did you do, then?'

'Nothing. I hesitated; I put off coming to an explanation with him – unfortunately until it was too late.'

'What do you mean by too late?'

'You shall hear. I ought to have told you that Richard Wardour is in the navy——'

'Indeed? I am more interested in him than ever. Well?'

'One spring day, Richard came to our house to take leave of us before he joined his ship. I thought he was gone, and I went into the next room. It was my own sitting-room, and it opened on to the garden.'

'Yes?'

'Richard must have been watching me. He suddenly appeared in the garden. Without waiting for me to invite him, he walked into the room. I was a little startled as well as surprised, but I managed to hide it. I said, "What is it, Mr Wardour?" He stepped close up to me; he said, in his quick, rough way: "Clara! I am going to the African coast. If I live, I shall come back promoted; and we both know what will happen then." He kissed me. I was half frightened, half angry. Before I could compose myself to say a word, he was out in the garden again – he was gone! I ought to have spoken, I know. It was not honourable, not kind towards *him*. You can't reproach me for my want of courage and frankness more bitterly than I reproach myself!'

'My dear child, I don't reproach you. I only think you might have written to him.'

'I did write.'

'Plainly?'

'Yes. I told him in so many words that he was deceiving himself, and that I could never marry him.'

'Plain enough, in all conscience! Having said that, surely you are not to blame? What are you fretting about now?'

'Suppose my letter has never reached him?'

'Why should you suppose anything of the sort?'

'What I wrote required an answer, Lucy – *asked* for an answer. The answer has never come. What is the plain conclusion? My letter has never reached him. And that *Atalanta* is expected back! Richard Wardour is returning to England – Richard Wardour will claim me as his wife! You wondered just now if I really meant what I said. Do you doubt it still?'

Mrs Crayford leaned back absently in her chair. For the first time since the conversation had begun she let a question pass without making a reply. The truth is, Mrs Crayford was thinking.

She saw Clara's position plainly; she understood the disturbing effect of it on the mind of a young girl. Still, making all allowances, she felt quite at a loss, so far, to account for Clara's excessive agitation. Her quick observing faculty had just detected that Clara's face showed no signs of relief, now that she had unburdened herself of her secret. There was something clearly under the surface here – something of importance, that still remained to be discovered. A shrewd doubt crossed Mrs Crayford's mind, and inspired the next words which she addressed to her young friend.

'My dear,' she said abruptly, 'have you told me all?'

Clara started as if the question terrified her. Feeling sure that she had the clue in her hand, Mrs Crayford deliberately repeated her question in another form of words. Instead of answering, Clara suddenly looked up. At the same moment a faint flush of colour appeared in her face for the first time.

Looking up instinctively on her side, Mrs Crayford became aware of the presence in the conservatory of a young gentleman who was claiming Clara as his partner in the coming waltz. Mrs Crayford fell into thinking once more. Had this young gentleman (she asked herself) anything to do with the untold end of the story? Was *this* the true secret of Clara Burnham's terror at the impending return of Richard Wardour? Mrs Crayford decided on putting her doubts to the test.

'A friend of yours, my dear?' she asked innocently. 'Suppose you introduce us to each other?'

Clara confusedly introduced the young gentleman.

'Mr Francis Aldersley, Lucy. Mr Aldersley belongs to the Arctic Expedition.'

'Attached to the expedition,' Mrs Crayford repeated. 'I am attached to the expedition too – in my way. I had better introduce myself, Mr Aldersley, as Clara seems to have forgotten to do it for me. I am Mrs Crayford. My husband is Lieutenant Crayford of the *Wanderer*. Do you belong to that ship?'

'I have not the honour, Mrs Crayford. I belong to the *Sea-Mew*.'

Mrs Crayford's superb eyes looked shrewdly backwards and forwards between Clara and Francis Aldersley, and saw the untold sequel to Clara's story. The young officer was a bright, handsome, gentleman-like lad – just the person to seriously complicate the difficulty with Richard Wardour! There was no time for making any further inquiries. The band had begun the prelude to the waltz, and Francis Aldersley was waiting for his partner. With a word of apology to the young man, Mrs Crayford drew Clara aside for a moment and spoke to her in a whisper.

'One word, my dear, before you return to the ball-room. It may sound conceited – after the little you have told me – but I think I understand your position *now* better than you do yourself. Do you want to hear my opinion?'

'I am longing to hear it, Lucy! I want your opinion; I want your advice.'

'You shall have both, in the plainest and the fewest words. First, my opinion: You have no choice but to come to an explanation with Mr Wardour as soon as he returns. Second, my advice: If you wish to make the explanation easy to both sides, take care that you make it in the character of a free woman.'

She laid a strong emphasis on the last three words, and looked pointedly at Francis Aldersley as she pronounced them. 'I won't keep you from your partner any longer, Clara,' she resumed, and led the way back to the ball-room.

CHAPTER III

The burden on Clara's mind weighs on it more heavily than ever after what Mrs Crayford has said to her. She is too unhappy to feel the inspiriting influence of the dance. After a turn round the room, she complains of fatigue. Mr Francis Aldersley looks at the conservatory (still as invitingly cool and empty as ever), leads her back to it, and places her on a seat among the shrubs. She tries – very feebly – to dismiss him.

'Don't let me keep you from dancing, Mr Aldersley.'

He seats himself by her side, and feasts his eyes on the lovely downcast face that dares not turn towards him. He whispers to her:

'Call me Frank.'

She longs to call him Frank – she loves him with all her heart. But Mrs Crayford's warning words are still in her mind. She never opens her lips. Her lover moves a little closer, and asks another favour. Men are all alike on these occasions. Silence invariably encourages them to try again.

'Clara! have you forgotten what I said at the concert yesterday? May I say it again?'

'No!'

'We shall sail to-morrow for the Arctic Seas. I may not return for years. Don't send me away without hope! Think of the long lonely time in the dark North! Make it a happy time for *me*.'

Though he speaks with the fervour of a man, he is little more than a lad; he is only twenty years old – and he is going to risk his young life on the frozen deep! Clara pities him as she never pitied any human creature before. He gently takes her hand. She tries to release it.

'What! Not even that little favour on the last night?'

Her faithful heart takes his part, in spite of her. Her hand remains in his, and feels its soft persuasive pressure. She is a lost woman. It is only a question of time now!

'Clara! do you love me?'

There is a pause. She shrinks from looking at him – she trembles with strange contradictory sensations of pleasure and pain. His arm steals round her; he repeats his question in a whisper; his lips almost touch her little rosy ear as he says it again:

'Do you love me?'

She closes her eyes faintly – she hears nothing but those words – feels nothing but his arm round her – forgets Mrs Crayford's warning – forgets Richard Wardour himself – turns suddenly, with a loving woman's desperate disregard of everything but her love, nestles her head on his bosom, and answers him in that way at last!

He lifts the beautiful drooping head – their lips meet in their first kiss – they are both in heaven – it is Clara who brings them back to earth again with a start – it is Clara who says, 'Oh! what have I done?' – as usual, when it is too late.

Frank answers the question.

'You have made me happy, my angel. Now, when I come back, I come back to make you my wife.'

She shudders. She remembers Richard Wardour again at those words.

'Mind!' she says, 'nobody is to know we are engaged till I permit you to mention it. Remember that!'

He promises to remember it. His arm tries to wind round her once more. No! She is mistress of herself; she can positively dismiss him now – after she has let him kiss her!

'Go!' she says. 'I want to see Mrs Crayford. Find her! Say I am here, waiting to speak to her. Go at once, Frank – for my sake!'

There is no alternative but to obey her. His eyes drink a last draught of her beauty. He hurries away on his errand – the happiest man in the room. Five minutes since, she was only his partner in the dance. He has spoken – and she has pledged herself to be his partner for life!

CHAPTER IV

It was not easy to find Mrs Crayford in the crowd. Searching here and searching there, Frank became conscious of a stranger, who appeared to be looking for somebody on his side. He was a dark, heavy-browed, strongly-built man; dressed in a shabby old naval officer's uniform. His manner – strikingly resolute and self-contained – was unmistakably the manner of a gentleman. He wound his way slowly through the crowd; stopping to look at every lady whom he passed, and then looking away again with a frown. Little by little he approached the conservatory – entered it, after a moment's reflection – detected the glimmer of a white dress in the distance, through the shrubs and flowers – advanced to get a nearer view of the lady – and burst into Clara's presence with a cry of delight.

She sprang to her feet. She stood before him speechless, motionless, struck to stone. All her life was in her eyes – the eyes which told her she was looking at Richard Wardour.

He was the first to speak.

'I am sorry I startled you, my darling. I forgot everything but the happiness of seeing you again. We only reached our moorings two hours since. I was some time inquiring after you, and some time getting my ticket, when they told me you were at the ball. Wish me joy, Clara! I am promoted. I have come back to make you my wife.'

A momentary change passed over the blank terror of her face. Her colour rose faintly, her lips moved. She abruptly put a question to him.

'Did you get my letter?'

He started. 'A letter from you? I never received it.'

The momentary animation died out of her face again. She drew back from him, and dropped into a chair. He advanced towards her, astonished and alarmed. She shrank in the chair – shrank, as if she was frightened of him.

'Clara! you have not even shaken hands with me! What does it mean?'

He paused, waiting, and watching her. She made no reply. A flash of the quick temper in him leapt up in his eyes. He repeated his last words in louder and sterner tones:

'What does it mean?'

She replied this time. His tone had hurt her – his tone had roused her sinking courage.

'It means, Mr Wardour, that you have been mistaken from the first.'

'How have I been mistaken?'

'You have been under a wrong impression, and you have given me no opportunity of setting you right.'

'In what way have I been wrong?'

'You have been too hasty and too confident about yourself and about me. You have entirely misunderstood me. I am grieved to distress you, but for your sake I must speak plainly. I am your friend always, Mr Wardour. I can never be your wife.'

He mechanically repeated the last words. He seemed to doubt whether he had heard her aright.

'You can never be my wife?'

'Never!'

'Why?'

There was no answer. She was incapable of telling him a falsehood. She was ashamed to tell him the truth.

He stooped over her, and suddenly possessed himself of her hand. Holding her hand firmly, he stooped a little lower, searching for the signs which might answer him in her face. His own face darkened slowly while he looked. He was beginning to suspect her, and he acknowledged it in his next words.

'Something has changed you towards me, Clara. Somebody has influenced you against me. Is it – you force me to ask the question – is it some other man?'

'You have no right to ask me that.'

He went on without noticing what she had said to him.

'Has that other man come between you and me? I speak plainly on my side. Speak plainly on yours.'

'I *have* spoken. I have nothing more to say.'

There was a pause. She saw the warning light which told of the fire within him, growing brighter and brighter in his eyes. She felt his grasp strengthening on her hand. She heard him appeal to her for the last time.

'Reflect,' he said, 'reflect before it is too late. Your silence will not serve you. If you persist in not answering me, I shall take your silence as a confession. Do you hear me?'

'I hear you.'

'Clara Burnham! I am not to be trifled with. Clara Burnham! I insist on the truth. Are you false to me?'

She resented that searching question with a woman's keen sense of the insult that is implied in doubting her to her face.

'Mr Wardour! you forget yourself when you call me to account in that way. I never encouraged you. I never gave you promise or pledge——'

He passionately interrupted her before she could say more.

'You have engaged yourself in my absence. Your words own it; your looks own it! You have engaged yourself to another man!'

'If I *have* engaged myself, what right have you to complain of it?' she answered firmly. 'What right have you to control my actions——?'

The next words died away on her lips. He suddenly dropped her hand. A marked change appeared in the expression of his eyes – a change which told her of the terrible passions that she had let loose in him. She read, dimly read, something in his face which made her tremble – not for herself, but for Frank.

Little by little the dark colour faded out of his face. His deep voice dropped suddenly to a low and quiet tone as he spoke the parting words.

'Say no more, Miss Burnham – you have said enough. I am answered; I am dismissed.' He paused, and stepping close up to her laid his hand on her arm.

'The time may come,' he said, 'when I shall forgive *you*. But the man who has robbed me of you shall rue the day when you and he first met.'

He turned, and left her.

A few minutes later, Mrs Crayford, entering the conservatory, was met by one of the attendants at the ball. The man stopped as if he wished to speak to her.

'What do you want?' she asked.

'I beg your pardon, ma'am. Do you happen to have a smelling-bottle about you? There is a young lady in the conservatory who is taken faint.'

BETWEEN THE SCENES

THE LANDING-STAGE

CHAPTER V

The morning of the next day – the morning on which the ships were to sail – came bright and breezy. Mrs Crayford, having arranged to follow her husband to the water-side and see the last of him before he embarked, entered Clara's room on her way out of the house, anxious to hear how her young friend had passed the night. To her astonishment, she found Clara had risen and was dressed, like herself, to go out.

'What does this mean, my dear? After what you suffered last night – after the shock of seeing that man – why don't you take my advice and rest in your bed?'

'I can't rest. I have not slept all night. Have you been out yet?'

'No.'

'Have you seen or heard anything of Richard Wardour?'

'What an extraordinary question!'

'Answer my question! Don't trifle with me!'

'Compose yourself, Clara. I have neither seen nor heard anything of Richard Wardour. Take my word for it, he is far enough away by this time.'

'No! He is here! He is near us! All night long the presentiment has pursued me – Frank and Richard Wardour will meet.'

'My dear child, what are you talking of? They are total strangers to each other.'

'Something will happen to bring them together. I feel it! I know it! They will meet; there will be a mortal quarrel between them, and I shall be to blame. Oh, Lucy! why didn't I take your advice? Why was I mad enough to let Frank know that I loved him? Are you going to the landing-stage? I am all ready; I must go with you.'

'You must not think of it, Clara. There will be crowding and confusion at the water-side. You are not strong enough to bear it. Wait – I won't be long away – wait till I come back.'

'I must, and will, go with you! Crowd! *He* will be among the crowd! Confusion! In the confusion *he* will find his way to Frank! Don't ask me to wait. I shall go mad if I wait. I shall not know a moment's ease until I have seen Frank with my own eyes safe in the boat which takes him to his ship. You have got your bonnet on; what are we stopping here for? Come! or I shall go without you. Look at the clock! We have not a moment to lose!'

It was useless to contend with her. Mrs Crayford yielded. The two women left the house together.

The landing-stage, as Mrs Crayford had predicted, was thronged with spectators. Not only the relatives and friends of the Arctic voyagers, but strangers as well, had assembled in large numbers to see the ships sail. Clara's eyes wandered affrightedly hither and thither among the strange faces in the crowd, searching for the one face that she dreaded to see, and not finding it. So completely were her nerves unstrung, that she startled with a cry of alarm on suddenly hearing Frank's voice behind her.

'The *Sea-Mew*'s boats are waiting,' he said. 'I must go, darling. How pale you are looking, Clara! Are you ill?'

She never answered. She questioned him with wild eyes and trembling lips.

'Has anything happened to you, Frank? anything out of the common?'

Frank laughed at the strange question.

'Anything out of the common?' he repeated. 'Nothing that I know of, except sailing for the Arctic Seas. That's out of the common, I suppose; isn't it?'

'Has anybody spoken to you since last night? Has any stranger followed you in the street?'

Frank turned in blank amazement to Mrs Crayford.

'What on earth does she mean?'

Mrs Crayford's lively invention supplied her with an answer on the spur of the moment.

'Do you believe in dreams, Frank? Of course you don't! Clara has been dreaming about you, and Clara is foolish enough to believe in dreams. That's all; it's not worth talking about. Hark! they are calling you. Say good-bye, or you will be too late for the boat.'

Frank took Clara's hand. Long afterwards – in the dark Arctic days, in the dreary Arctic nights – he remembered how coldly and how passively that hand lay in his.

'Courage, Clara!' he said gaily. 'A sailor's sweetheart must accustom herself to partings. The time will soon pass. Good-bye, my darling! Good-bye, my wife!'

He kissed the cold hand; he looked his last – for many a long year perhaps! – at the pale and beautiful face. How she loves me! he thought. How the parting distresses her! He still held her hand; he would have lingered longer, if Mrs Crayford had not wisely waived all ceremony and pushed him away.

The two ladies followed him at a safe distance through the crowd, and saw him step into the boat. The oars struck the water; Frank waved his cap to Clara. In a moment more a vessel at anchor hid the boat from view. They had seen the last of him on his way to the Frozen Deep!

'No Richard Wardour in the boat,' said Mrs Crayford. 'No Richard Wardour on the shore. Let this be a lesson to you, my dear. Never be foolish enough to believe in presentiments again.'

Clara's eyes still wandered suspiciously to and fro among the crowd.

'Are you not satisfied yet?' asked Mrs Crayford.

'No,' Clara answered. 'I am not satisfied yet.'

'What! still looking for him? This is really too absurd. Here is my husband coming. I shall tell him to call a cab and send you home.'

Clara drew back a few steps.

'I won't be in the way, Lucy, while you are taking leave of your good husband,' she said. 'I will wait here.'

'Wait here! What for?'

'For something which I may yet see. Or for something which I may still hear.'

'Richard Wardour?'

'Richard Wardour.'

Mrs Crayford turned to her husband without another word. Clara's infatuation was beyond the reach of remonstrance.

The boats of the *Wanderer* took the place at the landing-stage vacated by the boats of the *Sea-Mew*. A burst of cheering among the outer ranks of the crowd announced the arrival of the commander of the expedition on the scene. Captain Helding appeared, looking right and left for his first lieutenant. Finding Crayford with his wife, the captain made his apologies for interfering with his best grace.

'Give him up to his professional duties for one minute, Mrs Crayford, and you shall have him back again for half an hour. The Arctic Expedition is to blame, my dear lady – not the captain – for parting man and wife. In Crayford's place I should have left it to the bachelors to find the North-West Passage, and have stopped at home with you.'

Excusing himself in those bluntly complimentary terms, Captain Helding drew the lieutenant aside a few steps, accidentally taking a direction that led the two officers close to the place at which Clara was standing. Both the captain and the lieutenant were too completely absorbed in their professional duties to notice her. Neither the one nor the other had the faintest suspicion that she could, and did, hear every word of the talk that passed between them.

'You received my note this morning?' the captain began.

'Certainly, Captain Helding, or I should have been on board the ship before this.'

'I am going on board myself at once,' the captain proceeded. 'But I must ask you to keep your boat waiting for half an hour more. You will be all the longer with your wife, you know. I thought of that, Crayford.'

'I am much obliged to you, Captain Helding. I suppose there is some other reason for inverting the customary order of things, and keeping the lieutenant on shore after the captain is on board?'

'Quite true; there *is* another reason. I want you to wait for a volunteer who has just joined us.'

'A volunteer!'

'Yes; he has his outfit to get in a hurry, and he may be half an hour late.'

'It's rather a sudden appointment, isn't it?'

'No doubt. Very sudden.'

'And, pardon me, it's rather a long time (as we are situated) to keep the ships waiting for one man?'

'Quite true, again. But a man who is worth having is worth waiting for. This man is worth having; this man is worth his weight in gold to such an expedition as ours. Seasoned to all climates and all fatigues, a strong fellow, a brave fellow, a clever fellow – in short, an excellent officer. I know him well, or I should never have taken him. The country gets plenty of work out of my new volunteer, Crayford. He only returned yesterday from foreign service.'

'He only returned yesterday from foreign service, and he volunteers this morning to join the Arctic expedition! You astonish me.'

'I dare say I do; you can't be more astonished than I was when he presented himself at my hotel and told me what he wanted. "Why, my good fellow, you have just got home," I said; "are you weary of your freedom after only a few hours' experience of it?" His answer rather startled me. He said, "I am weary of my life, sir; I have come home and found a trouble to welcome me which goes near to break my heart. If I don't take refuge in absence and hard work, I am a lost man. Will you give me refuge?" That's what he said, Crayford, word for word.'

'Did you ask him to explain himself further?'

'Not I; I knew his value, and I took the poor devil on the spot without pestering him with any more questions. No need to ask him to explain himself; the facts speak for themselves in these cases. The old story, my good friend. There's a woman at the bottom of it, of course.'

Mrs Crayford, waiting for the return of her husband as patiently as she could, was startled by feeling a hand suddenly laid on her shoulder. She looked round and confronted Clara. Her first feeling of surprise changed instantly to alarm. Clara was trembling from head to foot.

'What is the matter? What has frightened you, my dear?'

'Lucy! I *have* heard of him!'

'Richard Wardour again?'

'Remember what I told you. I have heard every word of the conversation between Captain Helding and your husband. A man came to the Captain this morning and volunteered to join the *Wanderer*. The Captain has taken him. The man is Richard Wardour.'

'You don't mean it! Are you sure? Did you hear Captain Helding mention his name?'

'No.'

'Then how do you know it's Richard Wardour?'

'Don't ask me! I am as certain of it as that I am standing here! They are going away together, Lucy – away to the eternal ice and snow. My foreboding has come true! The two will meet – the man who is to marry me, and the man whose heart I have broken!'

'Your foreboding has *not* come true, Clara! The men have not met here – the men are not likely to meet elsewhere. They are appointed to separate ships. Frank belongs to the *Sea-Mew*, and Wardour to the *Wanderer*. See! Captain Helding has done. My husband is coming this way. Let me make sure. Let me speak to him.'

Lieutenant Crayford returned to his wife. She spoke to him instantly.

'William, you have got a new volunteer who joints the *Wanderer*?'

'What! you have been listening to the Captain and me?'

'I want to know his name.'

'How in the world did you manage to hear what we said to each other?'

'His name? has the Captain given you his name?'

'Don't excite yourself, my dear. Look! you are positively alarming Miss Burnham. The new volunteer is a perfect stranger to us. There is his name – last on the ship's list.'

Mrs Crayford snatched the list out of her husband's hand, and read the name:

'RICHARD WARDOUR.'

SECOND SCENE

THE HUT OF THE SEA-MEW

CHAPTER VI

Good-bye to England! Good-bye to inhabited and civilised regions of the earth!

Two years have passed since the voyagers sailed from their native shores. The enterprise has failed – the Arctic Expedition is lost and ice-locked in the Polar wastes. The good ships *Wanderer* and *Sea-Mew*, entombed in ice, will never ride the buoyant waters more. Stripped of their lighter timbers, both vessels have been used for the construction of huts, erected on the nearest land.

The largest of the two buildings which now shelter the lost men is occupied by the surviving officers and crew of the *Sea-Mew*. On one side of the principal room are the sleeping-berths and the fireplace. The other side discloses a broad doorway (closed by a canvas screen), which serves as a means of communication with an inner apartment, devoted to the superior officers. A hammock is slung to the rough raftered roof of the main room as an extra bed. A man, completely hidden by his bedclothes, is sleeping in the hammock. By the fireside there is a second man – supposed to be on the watch – fast asleep, poor wretch! at the present moment. Behind the sleeper stands an old cask, which serves for a table. The objects at present on the table are a pestle and mortar, and a saucepan full of the dry bones of animals. In plain words, the dinner for the day. By way of ornament to the dull brown walls, icicles appear in the crevices of the timber, gleaming at intervals in the red firelight. No wind whistles outside the lonely dwelling – no cry of bird or beast is heard. Indoors and out of doors the awful silence of the Polar desert reigns, for the moment, undisturbed.

CHAPTER VII

The first sound that broke the silence came from the inner apartment. An officer lifted the canvas screen in the hut of the *Sea-Mew* and entered the main room. Cold and privation had sadly thinned the ranks. The commander of the ship – Captain Ebsworth – was dangerously ill. The first lieutenant was dead. An officer of the *Wanderer* filled their places for the time, with Captain Helding's permission. The officer so employed was – Lieutenant Crayford.

He approached the man at the fireside and awakened him.

'Jump up, Bateson! It's your turn to be relieved.'

The relief appeared, rising from a heap of old sails at the back of the hut. Bateson vanished, yawning, to his bed. Lieutenant Crayford walked backwards and forwards briskly, trying what exercise would do towards warming his blood.

The pestle and mortar on the cask attracted his attention. He stopped and looked up at the man in the hammock.

'I must rouse the cook,' he said to himself, with a smile. 'That fellow little thinks how useful he is in keeping up my spirits. The most inveterate croaker and grumbler in the world – and yet, according to his own account, the only cheerful man in the whole ship's company. John Want! John Want! Rouse up, there!'

A head rose slowly out of the bedclothes, covered with a red night-cap. A melancholy nose rested itself on the edge of the hammock. A voice, worthy of the nose, expressed its opinion of the Arctic climate in these words:

'Lord! Lord! here's all my breath on my blanket. Icicles, if you please, sir, all round my mouth and all over my blanket. Every time I have snored I've frozen something. When a man gets the cold into him to that extent that he ices his own bed, it can't last much longer. Never mind! *I* don't grumble.'

Crayford tapped the saucepan of bones impatiently. John Want lowered himself to the floor – grumbling all the way – by a rope attached to the rafters at his bed head. Instead of approaching his superior officer and his saucepan he hobbled, shivering, to the fireplace, and held his chin as close as he possibly could over the fire. Crayford looked after him.

'Hullo! what are you doing there?'

'Thawing my beard, sir.'

'Come here directly, and set to work on these bones.'

John Want remained immovably attached to the fireplace, holding something else over the fire. Crayford began to lose his temper.

'What the devil are you about now?'

'Thawing my watch, sir. It's been under my pillow all night, and the cold has stopped it. Cheerful, wholesome, bracing sort of climate to live in, isn't it, sir? Never mind! *I* don't grumble.'

'No; we all know that. Look here! Are these bones pounded small enough?'

John Want suddenly approached the lieutenant, and looked at him with an appearance of the deepest interest.

'You'll excuse me, sir,' he said; 'how very hollow your voice sounds this morning.'

'Never mind my voice. The bones! the bones!'

'Yes, sir – the bones. They'll take a trifle more pounding. I'll do my best with them, sir, for your sake.'

'What do you mean?'

John Want shook his head, and looked at Crayford with a dreary smile.

'I don't think I shall have the honour of making much more bone soup for you, sir. Do you think yourself you'll last long, sir? I don't, saving your presence. I think about another week or ten days will do for us all. Never mind. *I* don't grumble.'

He poured the bones into the mortar and began to pound them – under protest. At the same moment a sailor appeared, entering from the inner hut.

'A message from Captain Ebsworth, sir.'

'Well?'

'The Captain is worse than ever with his freezing pains, sir. He wants to see you immediately.'

'I will go at once. Rouse the doctor.'

Answering in those terms, Crayford returned to the inner hut, followed by the sailor. John Want shook his head again, and smiled more drearily than ever.

'Rouse the doctor,' he repeated. 'Suppose the doctor should be frozen? He hadn't a ha'porth of warmth in him last night, and his voice sounded like a whisper in a speaking trumpet. Will the bones do now? Yes, the bones will do now. Into the saucepan with you,' cried John Want, suiting the action to the word, 'and flavour the hot water if you can! When I remember that I was once an apprentice at a pastrycook's – when I think of the gallons of turtle-soup that this hand has stirred up in a jolly hot kitchen – and when I find myself mixing bones and hot water for soup, and turning into ice as fast as I can, if I wasn't of a cheerful disposition I should feel inclined to grumble. John Want! John Want! whatever had you done with your natural senses, when you made up your mind to go to sea?'

A new voice hailed the cook, speaking from one of the bedplaces in the side of the hut. It was the voice of Francis Aldersley.

'Who's that croaking over the fire?'

'Croaking?' repeated John Want, with the air of a man who considered himself the object of a gratuitous insult. 'Croaking? You don't find your own voice at all altered for the worse – do you, Mr Frank? I don't give *him*,' John proceeded, speaking confidentially to himself, 'more than six hours to last. He's one of your grumblers.'

'What are you doing there?' asked Frank.

'I'm making bone soup, sir, and wondering why I ever went to sea.'

'Well, and why did you go to sea?'

'I'm not certain, Mr Frank. Sometimes I think it was natural perversity; sometimes I think it was false pride at getting over sea-sickness; sometimes I think it was reading Robinson Crusoe and books warning of me *not* to go to sea.'

Frank laughed. 'You're an odd fellow. What do you mean by false pride at getting over sea-sickness? Did you get over sea-sickness in some new way?'

John Want's dismal face brightened in spite of himself. Frank had recalled to the cook's memory one of the noteworthy passages in the cook's life.

'That's it, sir!' he said. 'If ever a man cured sea-sickness in a new way yet, I am that man – I got over it, Mr Frank, by dint of hard eating. I was a passenger on board a packet-boat, sir, when first I saw blue water. A nasty lopp of a sea came on at dinner-time, and I began to feel queer the moment the soup was put on the table. "Sick?" says the captain. "Rather, sir," says I. "Will you try my cure?" says the captain. "Certainly, sir," says I. "Is your heart in your mouth yet?" says the captain. "Not quite, sir," says I. "Mock-turtle soup," says the captain, and helps me. I swallow a couple of spoonfuls, and turn as white as a sheet. The captain cocks his eye at me. "Go on deck, sir," says he, "get rid of the soup, and then come back to the cabin." I got rid of the soup, and then came back to the cabin. "Cod's head-and-shoulders," says the captain, and helps me. "I can't stand it, sir," says I. "You must," says the captain, "because it's the cure." I crammed down a mouthful and turned paler than ever. "Go on deck," says the captain. "Get rid of the cod's head, and come back to the cabin." Off I go, and back I come. "Boiled leg of mutton and trimmings," says the captain, and helps me. "No fat, sir," says I. "Fat's the cure," says the captain, and makes me eat it. "Lean's the cure," says the captain, and makes me eat it. "Steady?" says the captain. "Sick," says I. "Go on deck," says the captain, "get rid of the boiled leg of mutton and trimmings, and come back to the cabin." Off I go, staggering – back I come, more dead than alive. "Devilled kidneys," says the captain. I shut my eyes, and get 'em down. "Cure's beginning," says the captain. "Mutton chop and pickles." I shut my eyes and got *them* down. "Broiled ham and cayenne pepper," says the captain. "Glass of stout and cranberry tart. Want to go on deck again?" "No, sir," says I. "Cure's done," says the captain. "Never you give in to your stomach, and your stomach will end in giving in to *you*."'

Having stated the moral purpose of his story in those unanswerable words, John Want took himself and his saucepan into the kitchen. A moment later Crayford returned to the hut, and astonished Frank Aldersley by an unexpected question.

'Have you anything in your berth, Frank, that you set a value on?'

Frank looked puzzled.

'Nothing that I set the smallest value on – when I am out of it,' he replied. 'What does your question mean?'

'We are almost as short of fuel as we are of provisions,' Crayford proceeded. 'Your berth will make good firing. I have directed Bateson to be here in ten minutes with his axe.'

'Very attentive and considerate on your part,' said Frank. 'What is to become of me, if you please, when Bateson has chopped my bed into firewood?'

'Can't you guess?'

'I suppose the cold has stupefied me. The riddle is beyond my reading. Suppose you give me a hint?'

'Certainly. There will be beds to spare soon – there is to be a change at last in our wretched lives here. Do you see it now?'

Frank's eyes sparkled. He sprang out of his berth and waved his fur cap in triumph.

'See it?' he exclaimed; 'of course I do! The exploring party is to start at last. Do I go with the expedition?'

'It is not very long since you were in the doctor's hands, Frank,' said Crayford, kindly. 'I doubt if you are strong enough yet to make one of the exploring party.'

'Strong enough or not,' returned Frank, 'any risk is better than pining and perishing here. Put me down, Crayford, among those who volunteer to go.'

'Volunteers will not be accepted in this case,' said Crayford. 'Captain Helding and Captain Ebsworth see serious objections, as we are situated, to that method of proceeding.'

'Do they mean to keep the appointments in their own hands?' asked Frank. 'I, for one, object to that.'

'Wait a little,' said Crayford. 'You were playing backgammon the other day with one of the officers. Does the board belong to him or to you?'

'It belongs to me. I have got it in my locker here. What do you want with it?'

'I want the dice and the box, for casting lots. The captains have arranged – most wisely, as I think – that Chance shall decide among us who goes with the expedition, and who stays behind in the huts. The officers and crew of the *Wanderer* will be here in a few minutes to cast the lots. Neither you nor any one can object to that way of settling the question. Officers and men alike take their chance together. Nobody can grumble.'

'*I* am quite satisfied,' said Frank. 'But I know of one man among the officers who is sure to make objections.'

'Who is the man?'

'You know him well enough too. The "Bear of the Expedition," Richard Wardour.'

'Frank! Frank! you have a bad habit of letting your tongue run away with you. Don't repeat that stupid nickname when you talk of my good friend, Richard Wardour.'

'Your good friend? Crayford! your liking for that man amazes me.'

Crayford laid his hand kindly on Frank's shoulder. Of all the officers of the 'Sea-Mew,' Crayford's favourite was Frank.

'Why should it amaze you?' he asked. 'What opportunities have *you* had of judging? You and Wardour have always belonged to different ships. I have never seen you in Wardour's society for five minutes together. How can *you* form a fair estimate of his character?'

'I take the general estimate of his character,' Frank answered. 'He has got his nickname because he is the most unpopular man in his ship. Nobody likes him – there must be some reason for that.'

'There is only one reason for it,' Crayford rejoined. 'Nobody understands Richard Wardour. I am not talking at random. Remember I sailed from England with him in the *Wanderer*, and I was only transferred to the *Sea-Mew* long after we were locked up in the ice. I was Richard Wardour's companion on board ship for months, and I learnt there to do him justice. Under all his outward defects, I tell you there beats a great and generous heart. Suspend your opinion, my lad, until you know my friend as well as I do. No more of this now. Give me the dice and the box.'

Frank opened his locker. At the same time the silence of the snowy waste outside was broken by a shouting of voices hailing the hut – '*Sea-Mew*, a-hoy!'

CHAPTER VIII

The sailor on watch opened the outer door. There, plodding over the ghastly white snow, were the officers of the *Wanderer* approaching the hut. There, scattered under the merciless black sky, were the crew, with the dogs and the sledges, waiting the word which was to start them on their perilous and doubtful journey.

Captain Helding of the *Wanderer*, accompanied by his officers, entered the hut – in high spirits at the prospect of a change. Behind them, lounging in slowly by himself, was a dark, sullen, heavy-browed man. He neither spoke nor offered his hand to anybody; he was the one person present who seemed to be perfectly indifferent to the fate in store for him. This was the man whom his brother officers had nicknamed the Bear of the Expedition. In other words – Richard Wardour.

Crayford advanced to welcome Captain Helding. Frank – remembering the friendly reproof which he had just received – passed over the other officers of the *Wanderer*, and made a special effort to be civil to Crayford's friend.

'Good morning, Mr Wardour,' he said. 'We may congratulate each other on the chance of leaving this horrible place.'

'*You* may think it horrible,' Wardour retorted. 'I like it.'

'Like it? Good heavens! why?'

'Because there are no women here.'

Frank turned to his brother officers, without making any further advances in the direction of Richard Wardour. The Bear of the Expedition was more unapproachable than ever.

In the meantime, the hut had become thronged by the able-bodied officers and men of the two ships. Captain Helding, standing in the midst of them, with Crayford by his side, proceeded to explain the purpose of the contemplated expedition to the audience which surrounded him.

He began in these words:–

'Brother officers and men of the *Wanderer* and *Sea-Mew*, it is my duty to tell you, very briefly, the reasons which have decided Captain Ebsworth and myself on despatching an exploring party in search of help. Without recalling all the hardships we have suffered for the last two years – the destruction, first of one of our ships, then of the other; the death of some of our bravest and best companions; the vain battles we have been fighting with the ice and snow, and boundless desolation of these inhospitable regions – without dwelling on these things, it is my duty to remind you that this, the last place in which we have taken refuge, is far beyond the track of any previous expedition, and that consequently our chance of being discovered by any rescuing parties that may be sent to look after us is, to say the least of it, a chance of the most uncertain kind. You all agree with me, gentlemen, so far?'

The officers (with the exception of Wardour, who stood apart in sullen silence) all agreed, so far.

The Captain went on.

'It is therefore urgently necessary that we should make another, and probably a last, effort to extricate ourselves. The winter is not far off, game is getting scarcer and scarcer, our stock of provisions is running low, and the sick – especially, I am sorry to say, the sick in the *Wanderer's* hut – are increasing in number day by day. We must look to our own lives, and to the lives of those who are dependent on us, and we have no time to lose.'

The officers echoed the words cheerfully.

'Right! right! No time to lose.'

Captain Helding resumed:

'The plan proposed is, that a detachment of the able-bodied officers and men among us should set forth this very day, and make another effort to reach the nearest inhabited settlements, from which help and provisions may be despatched to those who remain here. The new direction to be taken, and the various precautions to be adopted, are all drawn out ready. The only question now before us is – Who is to stop here, and who is to undertake the journey?'

The officers answered the question with one accord – 'Volunteers!'

The men echoed their officers. 'Aye, aye, volunteers.'

Wardour still preserved his sullen silence. Crayford noticed him, standing apart from the rest, and appealed to him personally.

'Do you say nothing?' he asked.

'Nothing,' Wardour answered. 'Go or stay, it's all one to me.'

'I hope you don't really mean that?' said Crayford.

'I do.'

'I am sorry to hear it, Wardour.'

Captain Helding answered the general suggestion in favour of volunteering by a question which instantly checked the rising enthusiasm of the meeting.

'Well,' he said, 'suppose we say volunteers. Who volunteers to stop in the huts?'

There was a dead silence. The officers and men looked at each other confusedly. The Captain continued.

'You see we can't settle it by volunteering. You all want to go. Every man among us who has the use of his limbs naturally wants to go. But what is to become of those who have *not* got the use of their limbs? Some of us must stay here and take care of the sick.'

Everybody admitted that this was true.

'So we get back again,' said the Captain, 'to the old question – Who among the able-bodied is to go, and who is to stay? Captain Ebsworth says, and I say, let chance decide it. Here are dice. The numbers run as high as twelve – double sixes. All who throw under six, stay; all who throw over six, go. Officers of the *Wanderer* and the *Sea-Mew*, do you agree to that way of meeting the difficulty?'

All the officers agreed – with the one exception of Wardour, who still kept silence.

'Men of the *Wanderer* and *Sea-Mew*, your officers agree to cast lots. Do you agree too?'

The men agreed without a dissentient voice. Crayford handed the box and the dice to Captain Helding.

'You throw first, sir. Under six, "Stay." Over six, "Go."'

Captain Helding cast the dice; the top of the cask serving for a table. He threw seven.

'Go,' said Crayford. 'I congratulate you, sir. Now for my own chance.' He cast the dice in his turn. Three. 'Stay! Ah, well! well! if I can do my duty and be of use to others, what does it matter whether I go or stay? Wardour, you are next, in the absence of your first lieutenant.'

Wardour prepared to cast without shaking the dice.

'Shake the box, man!' cried Crayford. 'Give yourself a chance of luck!'

Wardour persisted in letting the dice fall out carelessly, just as they lay in the box.

'Not I!' he muttered to himself. 'I've done with luck.' Saying those words, he threw down the empty box, and seated himself on the nearest chest, without looking to see how the dice had fallen.

Crayford examined them. 'Six!' he exclaimed. 'There! you have a second chance, in spite of yourself. You are neither under nor over – you throw again.'

'Bah!' growled the Bear. 'It's not worth the trouble of getting up for. Somebody else throw for me.' He suddenly looked at Frank. 'You! you have got what the women call a lucky face.'

Frank appealed to Crayford. 'Shall I?'

'Yes, if he wishes it,' said Crayford.

Frank cast the dice. 'Five! He stays! Wardour, I am sorry I have thrown against you.'

'Go or stay,' reiterated Wardour, 'it's all one to me. You will be luckier, young one, when you cast for yourself.'

Frank cast for himself.

'Eight. Hurrah! I go!'

'What did I tell you?' said Wardour. 'The chance was yours. You have thriven on my ill luck.'

He rose, as he spoke, to leave the hut. Crayford stopped him.

'Have you anything particular to do, Richard?'

'What has anybody to do here?'

'Wait a little, then. I want to speak to you when this business is over.'

'Are you going to give me any more good advice?'

'Don't look at me in that sour way, Richard. I am going to ask you a question about something which concerns yourself.'

Wardour yielded without a word more. He returned to his chest, and cynically composed himself to slumber. The casting of the lots went on rapidly among the officers and men. In another half hour chance had decided the question of 'Go' or 'Stay' for all alike. The men left the hut. The officers entered the inner apartment for a last conference with the bed-ridden captain of the *Sea-Mew*. Wardour and Crayford were left together, alone.

CHAPTER IX

Crayford touched his friend on the shoulder to rouse him. Wardour looked up, impatiently, with a frown.

'I was just asleep,' he said. 'Why do you wake me?'

'Look round you, Richard. We are alone.'

'Well – and what of that?'

'I wish to speak to you privately, and this is my opportunity. You have disappointed and surprised me to-day. Why did you say it was all one to you whether you went or stayed? Why are you the only man among us who seems to be perfectly indifferent whether we are rescued or not?'

'Can a man always give a reason for what is strange in his manner or his words?' Wardour retorted.

'He can try,' said Crayford quietly, 'when his friend asks him.'

Wardour's manner softened.

'That's true,' he said. 'I *will* try. Do you remember the first night at sea, when we sailed from England in the *Wanderer*?'

'As well as if it was yesterday.'

'A calm, still night,' the other went on, thoughtfully. 'No clouds, no stars. Nothing in the sky but the broad moon, and hardly a ripple to break the path of light she made in the quiet water. Mine was the middle watch that night. You came on deck, and found me alone——'

He stopped. Crayford took his hand, and finished the sentence for him.

'Alone – and in tears.'

'The last I shall ever shed.' Wardour added bitterly.

'Don't say that. There are times when a man is to be pitied, indeed, if he can shed no tears. Go on, Richard.'

Wardour proceeded – still following the old recollections, still preserving his gentler tones.

'I should have quarrelled with any other man who had surprised me at that moment,' he said. 'There was something, I suppose, in your voice, when you asked my pardon for disturbing me, that softened my heart. I told you I had met with a disappointment which had broken me for life. There was no need to explain further. The only hopeless wretchedness in this world is the wretchedness that women cause.'

'And the only unalloyed happiness,' said Crayford, 'the happiness that women bring.'

'That may be your experience of them,' Wardour answered. 'Mine is different. All the devotion, the patience, the humility, the worship that there is in man I laid at the feet of a woman. She accepted the offering as women do – accepted it easily, gracefully, unfeelingly – accepted it as a matter of course. I left England to win a high place in my profession before I dared to win *her*. I braved danger and faced death. I staked my life in the fever-swamps of Africa to gain the promotion that I only desired for her sake – and gained it. I came back to give her all, and to ask nothing in return but to rest my weary heart in the sunshine of her smile. And her own lips – the lips I had kissed at parting – told me that another man had robbed me of her. I spoke but few words when I heard that confession, and left her for ever. "The time may come," I told her, "when I shall forgive *you*. But the man who has robbed me of you shall rue the day when you and he first met." Don't ask me who he was! I have yet to discover him. The treachery had been kept secret; nobody could tell me where to find him; nobody could tell me who he was. What did it matter? When I had lived out the first agony, I could rely on myself – I could be patient and bide my time.'

'Your time? What time?'

'The time when I and that man shall meet, face to face. I knew it then; I know it now – it was written on my heart then, it is written on my heart now – we two shall meet and know each other! With that conviction strong within me, I volunteered for this service, as I would have volunteered for anything that set work and hardship and danger, like ramparts, between my misery and me. With that conviction strong within me still, I tell you it is no matter whether I stay here with the sick or go hence with the strong. I shall live till I have met that man! There is a day of reckoning appointed between us. Here in the freezing cold, or away in the deadly heat – in battle or in shipwreck – in the face of starvation, under the shadow of pestilence – I, though hundreds are falling round me, I shall live! live for the coming of one day! live for the meeting with one man!'

He stopped, trembling, body and soul, under the hold that his own terrible superstition had fastened on him. Crayford drew back in silent horror. Wardour noticed the action – he resented it – he appealed in defence of his one cherished conviction to Crayford's own experience of him.

'Look at me!' he cried. 'Look how I have lived and thriven, with the heartache gnawing at me at home, and the winds of the icy north whistling round me here! I am the strongest man among you. Why? I have fought through hardships that have laid the best-seasoned men of all our party on their backs. Why? What have *I* done, that my life should throb as bravely through every vein in my body at this minute, and in this deadly place, as ever it did in the wholesome breezes of home? What am I preserved for? I tell you again, for the coming of one day – for the meeting with one man.'

He paused once more. This time Crayford spoke.

'Richard!' he said, 'since we first met I have believed in your better nature, against all outward appearance. I have believed in you firmly, truly, as your brother might. You are putting that belief to a hard test. If your enemy had told me that you had ever talked as you talk now, that you had ever looked as you look now, I would have turned my back on him as the utterer of a vile calumny against a just, a brave, an upright man. Oh! my friend, my friend, if ever I have deserved well of you, put away those thoughts from your heart! Face me again with the stainless look of a man who has trampled under his feet the bloody superstitions of revenge, and knows them no more! Never, never let the time come when I cannot offer you my hand as I offer it now – to the man I can still admire, to the brother I can still love!'

The heart that no other voice could touch felt that appeal. The fierce eyes, the hard voice, softened under Crayford's influence. Richard Wardour's head sank on his breast.

'You are kinder to me than I deserve,' he said. 'Be kinder still, and forget what I have been talking about. No! no more about me; I am not worth it. We'll change the subject, and never go back to it again. Let's do something. Work, Crayford – that's the trule elixir of *our* life! Work, that stretches the muscles and sets the blood a-glowing. Work, that tires the body and rests the mind. Is there nothing in hand that I can do? Nothing to cut? nothing to carry?'

The door opened as he put the question. Bateson – appointed to chop Frank's bedplace into firing – appeared punctually with his axe. Wardour, without a word of warning, snatched the axe out of the man's hand.

'What was this wanted for?' he asked.

'To cut up Mr Aldersley's berth there into firing, sir.'

'I'll do it for you! I'll have it down in no time!' He turned to Crayford. 'You needn't be afraid about me, old friend. I am going to do the right thing. I am going to tire my body and rest my mind.'

The evil spirit in him was plainly subdued – for the time at least. Crayford took his hand in silence, and then (followed by Bateson) left him to his work.

CHAPTER X

Axe in hand, Wardour approached Frank's bedplace.

'If I could only cut the thoughts out of me,' he said to himself, 'as I am going to cut the billets out of this wood!' He attacked the bedplace with the axe like a man who well knew the use of his instrument. 'Oh, me,' he thought, sadly, 'if I had only been born a carpenter instead of a gentleman! A good axe, Master Bateson – I wonder where you got it? Something like a grip, my man, on this handle. Poor Crayford! his words stick in my throat. A fine fellow! a noble fellow! No use thinking, no use regretting; what is said *is* said. Work! work! work!'

Plank after plank fell out on the floor. He laughed over the easy task of destruction. 'Aha! young Aldersley! It doesn't take much to demolish your bedplace. I'll have it down! I would have the whole hut down, if they would only give me the chance of chopping at it!'

A long strip of wood fell to his axe – long enough to require cutting in two. He turned it, and stooped over it. Something caught his eye – letters carved in the wood. He looked closer. The letters were very faintly and badly cut. He could only make out the first three of them; and, even of those, he was not quite certain. They looked like C.L.A. – if they looked like anything. He threw down the strip of wood irritably.

'Damn the fellow (whoever he is) who cut this! Why should he carve *that* name, of all the names in the world?'

He paused, considering – then determined to go on again with his self-imposed labour. He was ashamed of his own outburst. He looked eagerly for the axe. 'Work, work! Nothing for it but work.' He found the axe, and went on again.

He cut out another plank.

He stopped, and looked at it suspiciously.

There was carving again on this plank. The letters F. and A. appeared on it.

He put down the axe. There were vague misgivings in him which he was not able to realise. The state of his own mind was fast becoming a puzzle to him.

'More carving,' he said to himself. 'That's the way these young idlers employ their long hours. F.A.? Those must be *his* initials – Frank Aldersley. Who carved the letters on the other plank? Frank Aldersley, too?'

He turned the piece of wood in his hand nearer to the light, and looked lower down it. More carving again, lower down! Under the initials F.A. were two more letters – C.B.

'C.B.?' he repeated to himself. 'His sweetheart's initials, I suppose? Of course – at his age – his sweetheart's initials.'

He paused once more. A spasm of inner pain showed the shadow of its mysterious passage outwardly on his face.

'*Her* cypher is C.B.,' he said, in low broken tones. 'C.B. – Clara Burnham.'

He waited, with the plank in his hand; repeating the name over and over again, as if it was a question he was putting to himself.

'Clara Burnham? Clara Burnham?'

He dropped the plank and turned deadly pale in a moment. His eyes wandered furtively backwards and forwards between the strip of wood on the floor and the half-demolished berth. 'O God! what has come to me now?' he said to himself, in a whisper. He snatched up the axe with a strange cry – something between rage and terror. He tried – fiercely, desperately tried – to go on with his work. No! strong as he was, he could not use the axe. His hands were helpless; they trembled incessantly. He went to the fire; he held his hands over it. They still trembled incessantly; they infected the rest of him. He shuddered all over. He knew fear. His own thoughts terrified him.

'Crayford!' he cried out. 'Crayford! come here, and let's go hunting.'

No friendly voice answered him. No friendly face showed itself at the door.

An interval passed, and there came over him another change. He recovered his self-possession almost as suddenly as he had lost it. A smile – a horrid, deforming, unnatural smile – spread slowly, stealthily, devilishly over his face. He left the fire; he put the axe away softly in a corner; he sat down in his old place, deliberately self-abandoned to a frenzy of vindictive joy. He had found the man! There, at the end of the world – there, at the last fight of the Arctic voyages against starvation and death – he had found the man!

The minutes passed.

He became conscious, on a sudden, of a freezing stream of air pouring into the room.

He turned, and saw Crayford opening the door of the hut. A man was behind him. Wardour rose eagerly and looked over Crayford's shoulder.

Was it – could it be – the man who had carved the letters on the plank? Yes! Frank Aldersley!

CHAPTER XI

'Still at work!' Crayford exclaimed, looking at the half-demolished bedplace. 'Give yourself a little rest, Richard. The exploring party is ready to start. If you wish to take leave of your brother officers before they go, you have no time to lose.'

He checked himself there, looking Wardour full in the face.

'Good heavens!' he cried, 'how pale you are. Has anything happened?'

Frank – searching in his locker for articles of clothing which he might require on the journey – looked round. He was startled, as Crayford had been startled, by the sudden change in Wardour since they had last seen him.

'Are you ill?' he asked. 'I hear you have been doing Bateson's work for him. Have you hurt yourself?'

Wardour suddenly moved his head, so as to hide his face from both Crayford and Frank. He took out his handkerchief, and wound it clumsily round his left hand.

'Yes,' he said, 'I hurt myself with the axe. It's nothing. Never mind. Pain always has a curious effect on me. I tell you it's nothing! don't notice it!'

He turned his face towards them again as suddenly as he had turned it away. He advanced a few steps, and addressed himself with an uneasy familiarity to Frank.

'I didn't answer you civilly when you spoke to me some little time since. I mean, when I first came in here, along with the rest of them. I apologize. Shake hands! How are you? Ready for the march?'

Frank met the oddly abrupt advance which had been made to him with perfect good humour.

'I am glad to be friends with you, Mr Wardour. I wish I was as well seasoned to fatigue as you are.'

Wardour burst into a hard, joyless, unnatural laugh.

'Not strong, eh? You don't look it. The dice had better have sent me away and kept you here. I never felt in better condition in my life.' He paused and added, with his eye on Frank, and with a strong emphasis on the words: 'We men of Kent are made of tough material.'

Frank advanced a step on his side, with a new interest in Richard Wardour.

'You come from Kent?' he said.

'Yes. From East Kent.' He waited a little once more, and looked hard at Frank. 'Do you know that part of the country?' he asked.

'I ought to know something about East Kent,' Frank answered. 'Some dear friends of mine once lived there.'

'Friends of yours?' Wardour repeated. 'One of the county families, I suppose?'

As he put the question he abruptly looked over his shoulder. He was standing between Crayford and Frank. Crayford, taking no part in the conversation, had been watching him and listening to him more and more attentively as that conversation went on. Within the last moment or two Wardour had become instinctively conscious of this. He resented Crayford's conduct with needless irritability.

'Why are you staring at me?' he asked.

'Why are you looking unlike yourself?' Crayford answered, quietly.

Wardour made no reply. He renewed the conversation with Frank.

'One of the county families?' he resumed. 'The Witherbys of Yew Grange, I daresay?'

'No,' said Frank; 'but friends of the Witherbys, very likely – the Burnhams.'

Desperately as he struggled to maintain it, Wardour's self-control failed him. He started violently. The clumsily-wound handkerchief fell off his hand. Still looking at him attentively, Crayford picked it up.

'There is your handkerchief, Richard,' he said. 'Strange!'

'What is strange?'

'You told us you had hurt yourself with the axe——'

'Well?'

'There is no blood on your handkerchief.'

Wardour snatched the handkerchief out of Crayford's hand, and, turning away, approached the outer door of the hut. 'No blood on the handkerchief,' he said to himself. 'There may be a stain or two when Crayford sees it again.' He stopped within a few paces of the door, and spoke to Crayford. 'You recommended me to take leave of my brother officers before it was too late,' he said. 'I am going to follow your advice.'

The door was opened from the outer side as he laid his hand on the lock.

One of the quartermasters of the *Wanderer* entered the hut.

'Is Captain Helding here, sir?' he asked, addressing himself to Wardour.

Wardour pointed to Crayford.

'The lieutenant will tell you,' he said.

Crayford advanced and questioned the quartermaster.

'What do you want with Captain Helding?' he asked.

'I have a report to make, sir. There has been an accident on the ice.'

'To one of your men?'

'No, sir. To one of our officers.'

Wardour – on the point of going out – paused when the quartermaster made that reply. For a moment he considered with himself. Then he walked slowly back to the part of the room in which Frank was standing. Crayford, directing the quartermaster, pointed to the arched doorway in the side of the hut.

'I am sorry to hear of the accident,' he said. 'You will find Captain Helding in that room.'

For the second time, with singular persistency, Wardour renewed the conversation with Frank.

'So you knew the Burnhams?' he said. 'What became of Clara when her father died?'

Frank's face flushed angrily on the instant.

'Clara?' he repeated. 'What authorises you to speak of Miss Burnham in that familiar manner?'

Wardour seized the opportunity of quarrelling with him.

'What right have you to ask?' he retorted coarsely.

Frank's blood was up. He forgot his promise to Clara to keep their engagement secret – he forgot everything but the unbridled insolence of Wardour's langauge and manner.

'A right which I insist on your respecting,' he answered. 'The right of being engaged to marry her.'

Crayford's steady eyes were still on the watch, and Wardour felt them on him. A little more, and Crayford might openly interfere. Even Wardour recognized, for once, the necessity of controlling his temper, cost him what it might. He made his apologies with overstrained politeness to Frank.

'Impossible to dispute such a right as yours,' he said. 'Perhaps you will excuse me when you know that I am one of Miss Burnham's old friends. My father and her father were neighbours. We have always met like brother and sister——'

Frank generously stopped the apology there.

'Say no more,' he interposed. 'I was in the wrong – I lost my temper. Pray forgive me.'

Wardour looked at him with a strange reluctant interest while he was speaking. Wardour asked an extraordinary question when he had done.

'Is she very fond of you?'

Frank burst out laughing.

'My dear fellow!' he said, 'come to our wedding, and judge for yourself.'

'Come to your wedding?' As he repeated the words Wardour stole one glance at Frank, which Frank (employed in buckling his knapsack) failed to see. Crayford noticed it – and Crayford's blood run cold. Comparing the words which Wardour had spoken to him while they were alone together with the words that had just passed in his presence, he could draw but one conclusion. The woman whom Wardour had loved and lost was – Clara Burnham. The man who had robbed him of her was Frank Aldersley. And Wardour had discovered it in the interval since they had last met. 'Thank God!' thought Crayford, 'the dice have parted them! Frank goes with the expedition, and Wardour stays behind with me.'

The reflection had barely occurred to him – Frank's thoughtless invitation to Wardour had just passed his lips – when the canvas screen over the doorway was drawn aside. Captain Helding and the officers who were to leave with the exploring party returned to the main room on their way out. Seeing Crayford, Captain Helding stopped to speak to him.

'I have a casualty to report,' said the captain, 'which diminishes our numbers by one. My second lieutenant, who was to have joined the exploring party, has had a fall on the ice. Judging by what the quartermaster tells me, I am afraid the poor fellow has broken his leg.'

'I will supply his place,' cried a voice at the other end of the hut.

Everybody looked round. The man who had spoken was Richard Wardour.

Crayford instantly interfered – so vehemently as to astonish all who knew him.

'No!' he said. Not you, Richard! not you!'

'Why not?' Wardour asked sternly.

'Why not, indeed?' added Captain Helding. 'Wardour is the very man to be useful on a long march. He is in perfect health, and he is the best shot among us. I was on the point of proposing him myself.'

Crayford failed to show his customary respect for his superior officer. He openly disputed the Captain's conclusion.

'Wardour has no right to volunteer,' he rejoined. 'It has been settled, Captain Helding, that chance shall decide who is to go and who is to stay.'

'And chance *has* decided it,' cried Wardour. 'Do you think we are going to cast the dice again, and give an officer of the *Sea-Mew* a chance of replacing an officer of the *Wanderer*? There is a vacancy in our party, not in yours; and we claim the right of filling it as we please. I volunteer, and my captain backs me. Whose authority is to keep me here after that?'

'Gently, Wardour,' said Captain Helding. 'A man who is in the right can afford to speak with moderation.' He turned to Crayford. 'You must admit yourself,' he continued, 'that Wardour is right this time. The missing man belongs to my command, and in common justice one of my officers ought to supply his place.'

It was impossible to dispute the matter further. The dullest man present could see that the Captain's reply was unanswerable. In sheer despair, Crayford took Frank's arm and led him aside a few steps. The last chance left of parting the two men was the chance of appealing to Frank.

'My dear boy,' he began, 'I want to say one friendly word to you on the subject of your health. I have already, if you remember, expressed my doubts whether you are strong enough to make one of an exploring party. I feel those doubts more strongly than ever at this moment. Will you take the advice of a friend who wishes you well?'

Wardour had followed Crayford. Wardour roughly interposed before Frank could reply.

'Let him alone!'

Crayford paid no heed to the interruption. He was too earnestly bent on withdrawing Frank from the expedition to notice anything that was said or done by the persons about him.

'Don't, pray don't, risk hardships which you are unfit to bear!' he went on entreatingly. 'Your place can be easily filled. Change your mind, Frank. Stay here with me.'

Again Wardour interfered. Again he called out, 'Leave him alone!' more roughly than ever. Still deaf and blind to every consideration but one, Crayford pressed his entreaties on Frank.

'You owned yourself just now that you were not well seasoned to fatigue,' he persisted. 'You feel (you *must* feel) how weak that last illness has left you? You know (I am sure you know) how unfit you are to brave exposure to cold and long marches over the snow.'

Irritated beyond endurance by Crayford's obstinacy, seeing, or thinking he saw, signs of yielding in Frank's face, Wardour so far forgot himself as to seize Crayford by the arm, and attempt to drag him away from Frank. Crayford turned and looked at him.

'Richard,' he said, very quietly, 'you are not yourself. I pity you. Drop your hand.'

Wardour relaxed his hold with something of the sullen submission of a wild animal to his keeper. The momentary silence which followed gave Frank an opportunity of speaking at last.

'I am gratefully sensible, Crayford,' he began, 'of the interest which you take in me——'

'And you will follow my advice?' Crayford interposed eagerly.

'My mind is made up, old friend,' Frank answered, firmly and sadly. 'Forgive me for disappointing you. I am appointed to the expedition. With the expedition I go.' He moved nearer to Wardour. In his innocence of all suspicion, he clapped Wardour heartily on the shoulder. 'When I feel the fatigue,' said poor simple Frank, 'you will help me, comrade – won't you? Come along!'

Wardour snatched his gun out of the hands of the sailor who was carrying it for him. His dark face became suddenly irradiated with a terrible joy.

'Come!' he said. 'Over the snow and over the ice! Come! where no human footsteps have ever trodden and where no human trace is ever left.'

Blindly, instinctively, Crayford made an effort to part them. His brother officers, standing near, pulled him back. They looked at each other anxiously. The merciless cold, striking its victims in various ways, had struck in some instances at their reason first. Everybody loved Crayford. Was he, too, going on the dark way that others had taken before him? They forced him to seat himself on one of the lockers. 'Steady, old fellow!' they said kindly – 'steady!' Crayford yielded, writhing inwardly under the sense of his own helplessness. What in God's name could he do? Could he denounce Wardour to Captain Helding on bare suspicion – without so much as the shadow of a proof to justify what he said? The Captain would decline to insult one of his officers by even mentioning the monstrous accusation to him. The Captain would conclude, as others had already concluded, that Crayford's mind was giving way under stress of cold and privation. No hope – literally, no hope now but in the numbers of the expedition. Officers and men, they all liked Frank. As long as they could stir hand or foot they would help him on the way – they would see that no harm came to him.

The word of command was given; the door was thrown open; the hut emptied rapidly. Over the merciless white snow – under the merciless black sky – the exploring party began to move. The sick and helpless men, whose last hope of rescue centred in their departing messmates, cheered faintly. Some few whose days were numbered sobbed and cried like women. Frank's voice faltered as he turned back at the door to say his last words to the friend who had been a father to him.

'God bless you, Crayford!'

Crayford broke away from the officers near him, and, hurrying forward, seized Frank by both hands. Crayford held him as if he would never let him go.

'God preserve you, Frank! I would give all I have in the world to be with you. Good-bye! Good-bye!'

Frank waved his hand – dashed away the tears that were gathering in his eyes – and hurried out. Crayford called after him, the last, the only, warning that he could give:

'While you can stand, keep with the main body, Frank!'

Wardour, waiting till the last – Wardour, following Frank through the snow-drift – stopped, stepped back, and answered Crayford at the door:

'While he can stand, he keeps with Me.'

THIRD SCENE

THE ICEBERG

CHAPTER XII

Alone! alone on the Frozen Deep!

The Arctic sun is rising dimly in the dreary sky. The beams of the cold northern moon, mingling strangely with the dawning light, clothe the snowy plains in hues of livid grey. An ice-field on the far horizon is moving slowly southward in the spectral light. Nearer, a stream of open water rolls its slow black waves past the edges of the ice. Nearer still, following the drift, an iceberg rears its crags and pinnacles to the sky; here, glittering in the moonbeams; there, looming dim and ghostlike in the ashy light.

Midway on the long sweep of the lower slope of the iceberg, what objects rise and break the desolate monotony of the scene? In this awful solitude can signs appear which tell of human life? Yes! The black outline of a boat just shows itself, hauled up on the berg. In an ice-cavern behind the boat the last red embers of a dying fire flicker from time to time over the figures of two men. One is seated, resting his back against the side of the cavern. The other lies prostrate with his head on his comrade's knee. The first of these men is awake, and thinking. The second reclines, with his still white face turned up to the sky – sleeping or dead. Days and days since, these two have fallen behind on the march of the expedition of relief. Days and days since, these two have been given up by their weary and failing companions as doomed and lost. He who sits thinking is Richard Wardour. He who lies sleeping or dead is Frank Aldersley.

The iceberg drifts slowly, over the black water, through the ashy light. Minute by minute the dying fire sinks. Minute by minute the deathly cold creeps nearer and nearer to the lost men.

Richard Wardour rouses himself from his thoughts, looks at the still white face beneath him, and places his hand on Frank's heart. It still beats feebly. Give him his share of the food and fuel still stored in the boat, and Frank may live through it. Leave him neglected where he lies, and his death is a question of hours, perhaps minutes – who knows?

Richard Wardour lifts the sleeper's head and rests it against the cavern side. He goes to the boat and returns with a billet of wood. He stoops to place the wood on the fire, and stops. Frank is dreaming, and murmuring in his dream. A woman's name passes his lips. Frank is in England again – at the ball – whispering to Clara the confession of his love.

Over Richard Wardour's face there passes the shadow of a deadly thought. He rises from the fire; he takes the wood back to the boat. His iron strength is shaken, but it still holds out. They are drifting nearer and nearer to the open sea. He can launch the boat without help; he can take the food and the fuel with him. The sleeper on the iceberg is the man who has robbed him of Clara – who has wrecked the hope and the happiness of his life. Leave the man in his sleep, and let him die!

So the tempter whispers. Richard Wardour tries his strength on the boat. It moves; he has got it under control. He stops and looks round. Beyond him is the open sea. Beneath him is the man who has robbed him of Clara. The shadow of the deadly thought grows and darkens over his face. He waits with his hands on the boat – waits and thinks.

The iceberg drifts slowly, over the black water, through the ashy light. Minute by minute the dying fire sinks. Minute by minute the deathly cold creeps nearer to the sleeping man. And still Richard Wardour waits – waits and thinks.

FOURTH SCENE

THE GARDEN

CHAPTER XIII

The spring has come. The air of the April night just lifts the leaves of the sleeping flowers. The moon is queen in the cloudless and starless sky. The stillness of the midnight hour is abroad, over land and over sea.

In a villa on the westward shore of the Isle of Wight, the glass doors which lead from the drawing-room to the garden are yet open. The shaded lamp yet burns on the table. A lady sits by the lamp, reading. From time to time she looks out into the garden, and sees the white-robed figure of a young girl pacing slowly to and fro in the soft brightness of the moonlight on the lawn. Sorrow and suspense have set their mark on the lady. Not rivals only, but friends who formerly admired her, agree now that she looks worn and aged. The more merciful judgment of others remarks, with equal truth, that her eyes, her hair, her simple grace and grandeur of movement have lost but little of their olden charms. The truth lies, as usual, between the two extremes. In spite of sorrow and suffering, Mrs Crayford is the beautiful Mrs Crayford still.

The delicious silence of the hour is softly disturbed by the voice of the younger lady in the garden.

'Go to the piano, Lucy. It is a night for music. Play something that is worthy of the night.'

Mrs Crayford looks round at the clock on the mantelpiece.

'My dear Clara, it is past twelve! Remember what the doctor told you. You ought to have been in bed an hour ago.'

'Half an hour, Lucy – give me half an hour more! Look at the moonlight on the sea. Is it possible to go to bed on such a night as this? Play something, Lucy – something spiritual and divine.'

Earnestly pleading with her friend, Clara advances towards the window. She too has suffered under the wasting influences of suspense. Her face has lost its youthful freshness; no delicate flush of colour rises on it when she speaks. The soft grey eyes which won Frank's heart in the bygone time are sadly altered now. In repose they have a dimmed and wearied look. In action they are wild and restless, like eyes suddenly wakened from startling dreams. Robed in white, her soft brown hair hanging loosely over her shoulders, there is something weird and ghostlike in the girl, as she moves nearer and nearer to the window in the full light of the moon – pleading for music that shall be worthy of the mystery and the beauty of the night.

'Will you come in here if I play to you?' Mrs Crayford asks. 'It is a risk, my love, to be out in the night air.'

'No! no! I like it. Play – while I am out here, looking at the sea. It quiets me; it comforts me; it does me good.'

She glides back, ghostlike over the lawn. Mrs Crayford rises and puts down the volume that she has been reading. It is a record of explorations in the Arctic seas. The time has gone by when the two lonely women could take an interest in subjects not connected with their own anxieties. Now, when hope is fast failing them – now, when their last news of the *Wanderer* and the *Sea-Mew* is news that is more than two years old – they can read of nothing, they can think of nothing, but dangers and discoveries, losses and rescues in the terrible Polar seas.

Unwillingly, Mrs Crayford puts her book aside and goes to the piano – Mozart's 'Air in A, with Variations,' lies open on the instrument. One after another she plays the lovely melodies, so simply, so purely beautiful, of that unpretending and unrivalled work. At the close of the ninth variation (Clara's favourite) she pauses, and turns towards the garden.

'Shall I stop there?' she asks.

There is no answer. Has Clara wandered away out of hearing of the music that she loves – the music that harmonises so subtly with the tender beauty of the night? Mrs Crayford rises and advances to the window.

No! there is the white figure standing alone on the slope of the lawn – the head turned away from the house; the face looking out over the calm sea, whose gently rippling waters end in the dim line on the horizon, which is the line of the Hampshire coast.

Mrs Crayford advances as far as the path before the window and calls to her.

'Clara!'

Again there is no answer. The white figure still stands immovably in its place.

With signs of distress in her face, but with no appearance of alarm, Mrs Crayford returns to the room. Her own sad experience tells her what has happened. She summons the servants, and directs them to wait in the drawing-room until she calls to them. This done, she returns to the garden, and approaches the mysterious figure on the lawn.

Dead to the outer world, as if she lay already in her grave – insensible to touch, insensible to sound, motionless as stone, cold as stone – Clara

stands on the moonlit lawn, facing the seaward view. Mrs Crayford waits
at her side, patiently watching for the change which she knows is to
come. 'Catalepsy,' as some call it – hysteria, as others say – this alone is
certain, the same interval always passes; the same change always appears.

It comes now. Not a change in her eyes; they still remain wide open,
fixed, and glassy. The first movement is a movement of her hands. They
rise slowly from her side, and waver in the air like the hands of a person
groping in the dark. Another interval – and the movement spreads to her
lips; they part and tremble. A few minutes more, and words begin to
drop, one by one, from those parted lips – words spoken in a lost vacant
tone, as if she is talking in her sleep.

Mrs Crayford looks back at the house. Sad experience makes her
suspicious of the servants' curiosity. Sad experience has long since warned
her that the servants are not to be trusted within hearing of the wild
words which Clara speaks in the trance. Has any one of them ventured
into the garden? No. They are out of hearing at the window, waiting for
the signal which tells them that their help is needed.

Turning towards Clara once more, Mrs Crayford hears the vacantly-
uttered words falling faster and faster from her lips.

'Frank! Frank! Frank! Don't drop behind – don't trust Richard
Wardour. While you can stand, keep with the other men, Frank!'

(The farewell warning of Crayford in the solitudes of the Frozen Deep,
repeated by Clara in the garden of her English home!)

A moment of silence follows, and in that moment the vision has
changed. She sees him on the iceberg now, at the mercy of the bitterest
enemy he has on earth. She sees him drifting, over the black water,
through the ashy light.

'Wake, Frank! wake and defend yourself! Richard Wardour knows that
I love you. Richard Wardour's vengeance will take your life! Wake,
Frank! – wake! You are drifting to your death!' A low groan of horror
bursts from her, sinister and terrible to hear. 'Drifting! drifting!' she
whispers to herself; 'drifting to his death!'

Her glassy eyes suddenly soften, then close. A long shudder runs
through her. A faint flush shows itself on the deadly pallor of her face,
and fades again. Her limbs fail her. She sinks into Mrs Crayford's arms.

The servants, answering the call for help, carry her into the house.
They lay her insensible on her bed. After an hour or more, her eyes open
again – this time with the light of life in them – open, and rest languidly
on her friend sitting by the bedside.

'I have had a dreadful dream,' she murmurs faintly. 'Am I ill, Lucy? I
feel so weak.'

Even as she says the words sleep, gentle, natural sleep, takes her
suddenly, as it takes young children weary with their play. Though it is all

over now, though no further watching is required, Mrs Crayford still keeps her place by the bedside, too anxious and too wakeful to retire to her own room.

On other occasions she is accustomed to dismiss from her mind the words which drop from Clara in the trance. This time the effort to dismiss them is beyond her power. The words haunt her. Vainly she recalls to memory all that the doctors have said to her in speaking of Clara in the state of trance. 'What she vaguely dreads for the lost man whom she loves, is mingled in her mind with what she is constantly reading of trials, dangers, and escapes in the Arctic Seas. The most startling things that she may say or do are all attributable to this cause, and may be explained in this way.' So the doctors have spoken; and, thus far, Mrs Crayford has shared their view. It is only to-night that the girl's words ring in her ear with a strange prophetic sound in them. It is only to-night that she asks herself: 'Is Clara present, in the spirit, with our loved and lost ones in the lonely North? Can mortal vision see the dead and living in the solitudes of the Frozen Deep?'

CHAPTER XIV

The night had passed.

Far and near, the garden-view looked its gayest and brightest in the light of the noonday sun. The cheering sounds which tell of life and action were audible all round the villa. From the garden of the nearest house rose the voices of children at play. Along the road at the back sounded the roll of wheels, as carts and carriages passed at intervals. Out on the blue sea the distant splash of the paddles, the distant thump of the engines, told from time to time of the passage of steamers, entering or leaving the strait between the island and the mainland. In the trees the birds sang gaily among the rustling leaves. In the house the women-servants were laughing over some jest or story that cheered them at their work. It was a lively and pleasant time – a bright enjoyable day.

The two ladies were out together, resting on a garden seat, after a walk round the grounds.

They exchanged a few trivial words relating to the beauty of the day, and then said no more. Possessing the same consciousness of what she had seen in the trance which persons in general possess of what they have seen in a dream – believing in the vision as a supernatural revelation – Clara's worst forebodings were now, to her mind, realised as truths. Her last faint hope of ever seeing Frank again was now at an end. Intimate experience of her told Mrs Crayford what was passing in

Clara's mind, and warned her that the attempt to reason and remonstrate would be little better than a voluntary waste of words and time. The disposition which she had herself felt, on the prevoius night, to attach a superstitious importance to the words that Clara had spoken in the trance had vanished with the return of the morning. Rest and reflection had quieted her mind, and had restored the composing influence of her sober sense. Sympathizing with Clara in all besides, she had no sympathy, as they sat together in the pleasant sunshine, with Clara's gloomy despair of the future. She, who could still hope, had nothing to say to the sad companion who had done with hope. So the quiet minutes succeeded each other, and the two friends sat side by side in silence.

An hour passed – and the gate-bell of the villa rang.

They both started – they both knew the ring. It was the hour when the postman brought their newspapers from London. In past days, what hundreds on hundreds of times they had torn off the cover which enclosed the newspaper, and looked at the same column with the same weary mingling of hope and despair! There to-day – as it was yesterday; as it would be, if they lived, to-morrow – there was the servant with Lucy's newspaper and Clara's newspaper in his hand! Would both of them do again to-day what both of them had done so often in the days that were gone?

No! Mrs Crayford removed the cover from her newspaper as usual. Clara laid *her* newspaper aside, unopened, on the garden seat.

In silence Mrs Crayford looked where she always looked, at the column devoted to the Latest Intelligence from foreign parts. The instant her eye fell on the page she started with a loud cry of joy. The newspaper fell from her trembling hand. She caught Clara in her arms. 'Oh, my darling! my darling! news of them at last.'

Without answering, without the slightest change in look or manner, Clara took the newspaper from the ground, and read the top line in the column, printed in capital letters.

THE ARCTIC EXPEDITION

She waited, and looked at Mrs Crayford.

'Can you bear to hear it, Lucy,' she asked, 'if I read it aloud?'

Mrs Crayford was too agitated to answer in words. She signed impatiently to Clara to go on.

Clara read the news which followed the heading in capital letters. Thus it ran:

'The following intelligence from St John's, Newfoundland, has reached us for publication. The whaling vessel *Blythewood* is reported to have met with the surviving officers and men of the expedition in Davis Stait. Many are stated to be dead, and some are supposed to be missing. The

list of the saved, as collected by the people of the whaler, is not vouched
for as being absolutely correct, the circumstances having been adverse to
investigation. The vessel was pressed for time; and the members of the
expedition, all more or less suffering from exhaustion, were not in a
position to give the necessary assistance to inquiry. Further particulars
may be looked for by the next mail.'

The list of the survivors followed, beginning with the officers in the
order of their rank. They both read the list together. The first name was
Captain Helding. The second was Lieutenant Crayford.

There, the wife's joy overpowered her. After a pause, she put her arms
round Clara's waist, and spoke to her.

'Oh, my love!' she murmured, 'are you as happy as I am? Is Frank's
name there too? The tears are in my eyes. Read for me – I can't read for
myself.'

The answer came, in still sad tones:

'I have read as far as your husband's name. I have no need to read
further.'

Mrs Crayford dashed the tears from her eyes, steadied herself, and
looked at the newspaper.

On the list of the survivors the search was vain. Frank's name was not
among them. On a second list, headed 'Dead or Missing,' the two first
names that appeared were:

FRANCIS ALDERSLEY
RICHARD WARDOUR

In speechless distress and dismay Mrs Crayford looked at Clara. Had
she force enough, in her feeble health, to sustain the shock that had fallen
on her? Yes! She bore it with a strange unnatural resignation; she looked,
she spoke, with the sad self-possession of despair.

'I was prepared for it,' she said. 'I saw them in the spirit last night.
Richard Wardour has discovered the truth, and Frank has paid the
penalty with his life – and I, I alone, am to blame.' She shuddered, and
put her hand on her heart. 'We shall not be long parted, Lucy; I shall go
to him. He will not return to me.'

Those words were spoken with a calm certainty of conviction that was
terrible to see. 'I have no more to say,' she added, after a moment, and
rose to return to the house. Mrs Crayford caught her by the hand, and
forced her to take her seat again.

'Don't look at me, don't speak to me, in that horrible manner!' she
exclaimed. 'Clara, it is unworthy of a reasonable being, it is doubting the
mercy of God, to say what you have just said. Look at the newspaper
again. See! They tell you plainly that their information is not to be
depended upon – they warn you to wait for further particulars. The very

words at the top of the list show how little they know of the truth. "Dead, *or* missing!" On their own showing it is quite as likely that Frank is missing as that Frank is dead. For all you know, the next mail may bring a letter from him. Are you listening to me?'

'Yes.'

'Can you deny what I say?'

'No.'

'"Yes!" "No!" Is that the way to answer me when I am so distressed and so anxious about you?'

'I am sorry I spoke as I did, Lucy. We look at some subjects in very different ways. I don't dispute, dear, that yours is the reasonable view.'

'You don't dispute?' retorted Mrs Crayford warmly. 'No! you do what is worse – you believe in your own opinion – you persist in your own conclusion – with the newspaper before you! Do you, or do you not, believe the newspaper?'

'I believe in what I saw last night.'

'In what you saw last night! You, an educated woman, a clever woman, believing in a vision of your own fancy – a mere dream! I wonder you are not ashamed to acknowledge it!'

'Call it a dream if you like, Lucy. I have had other dreams, at other times, and I have known them to be fulfilled.'

'Yes!' said Mrs Crayford. 'For once in a way they may have been fulfilled, by chance – and you notice it, and remember it, and pin your faith on it. Come, Clara, be honest! What about the occasions when the chance has been against you, and your dreams have *not* been fulfilled? You superstitious people are all alike. You conveniently forget when your dreams and your presentiments prove false. For my sake, dear, if not for your own,' she continued, in gentler and tenderer tones, 'try to be more reasonable and more hopeful. Don't lose your trust in the future and your trust in God. God, who has saved my husband, can save Frank. While there is doubt there is hope. Don't embitter my happiness, Clara! Try to think as I think – if it is only to show that you love me.'

She put her arms round the girl's neck and kissed her. Clara returned the kiss; Clara answered sadly and submissively:

'I do love you, Lucy. I *will* try.'

Having answered in those terms, she sighed to herself, and said no more. It would have been plain, only too plain, to far less observant eyes than Mrs Crayford's that no salutary impression had been produced on her. She had ceased to defend her own way of thinking, she spoke of it no more; but there was the terrible conviction of Frank's death at Wardour's hands rooted as firmly as ever in her mind! Discouraged and distressed, Mrs Crayford left her, and walked back towards the house.

CHAPTER XV

At the drawing-room window of the villa there appeared a polite little man, with bright intelligent eyes and cheerful sociable manners. Neatly dressed in professional black, he stood, self-proclaimed, a prosperous country doctor – successful and popular in a wide circle of patients and friends. As Mrs Crayford approached him, he stepped out briskly to meet her on the lawn, with both hands extended in courteous and cordial greeting.

'My dear madam, accept my heartfelt congratulations!' cried the doctor. 'I have seen the good news in the paper; and I could hardly feel more rejoiced than I do now if I had the honour of knowing Lieutenant Crayford personally. We mean to celebrate the occasion at home. I said to my wife before I came out, "A bottle of the old Madeira at dinner to-day, mind! – to drink the Lieutenant's health; God bless him!" And how is our interesting patient? The news is not altogether what we could wish, so far as she is concerned. I felt a little anxious, to tell you the truth, about the effect of it; and I have paid my visit to-day before my usual time. Not that I take a gloomy view of the news myself. No! There is clearly a doubt about the correctness of the information, so far as Mr Aldersley is concerned – and that is a point, a great point, in Mr Aldersley's favour. I give him the benefit of the doubt, as the lawyers say. Does Miss Burnham give him the benefit of the doubt too? I hardly dare hope it, I confess.'

'Miss Burnham has grieved and alarmed me,' Mrs Crayford answered. 'I was just thinking of sending for you, when we met here.'

With those introductory words, she told the doctor exactly what had happened; repeating, not only the conversation of that morning between Clara and herself, but also the words which had fallen from Clara in the trance of the past night.

The doctor listened attentively. Little by little, its easy smiling composure vanished from his face as Mrs Crayford went on, and left him completely transformed into a grave and thoughtful man.

'Let us go and look at her,' he said.

He seated himself by Clara's side, and carefully studied her face, with his hand on her pulse. There was no sympathy here between the dreamy mystical temperament of the patient and the downright practical character of the doctor. Clara secretly disliked her medical attendant. She submitted impatiently to the close investigation of which he made her the object. He questioned her, and she answered irritably. Advancing a step further (the doctor was not easily discouraged) he adverted to the news of the Expedition, and took up the tone of remonstrance which had been already adopted by Mrs Crayford. Clara declined to discuss the question. She rose with formal politeness, and requested permission to return to the house. The doctor attempted no further resistance. 'By all means, Miss Burnham,' he answered, resignedly – having first cast a look at Mrs Crayford which said plainly, 'Stay here with me.' Clara bowed her acknowledgments in cold silence, and left them together. The doctor's bright eyes followed the girl's wasted, yet still graceful, figure, as it slowly receded from view, with an expression of grave anxiety, which Mrs Crayford noticed with grave misgiving on her side. He said nothing until Clara had disappeared under the verandah which ran round the garden side of the house.

'I think you told me,' he began, 'that Miss Burnham has neither father nor mother living?'

'Yes. Miss Burnham is an orphan.'

'Has she any near relatives?'

'No. You may speak to me as her guardian and her friend. Are you alarmed about her?'

'I am seriously alarmed. It is only two days since I called here last – and I see a marked change in her for the worse. Physically and morally a change for the worse. Don't needlessly alarm yourself! The case is not, I trust, entirely beyond the reach of remedy. The great hope for us is the hope that Mr Aldersley may still be living. In that event, I should feel no misgivings about the future. Her marriage would make a healthy and a happy woman of her. But, as things are, I own I dread that settled conviction in her mind that Mr Aldersley is dead, and that her own death is soon to follow. In her present state of health, that idea (haunting her, as it certainly will, night and day) will have its influence on her body as well as on her mind. Unless we can check the mischief, her last reserves of strength will give way. If you wish for other advice by all means send for it. You have my opinion.'

'I am quite satisfied with your opinion,' Mrs Crayford replied. 'It is your advice I want. For God's sake tell me what can we do?'

'We can try a complete change,' said the doctor. 'We can remove her at once from this place.'

'She will refuse to leave it,' Mrs Crayford rejoined. 'I have more than once proposed a change to her – and she always says No.'

The doctor paused for a moment, like a man collecting his thoughts.

'I heard something on my way here,' he proceeded, 'which suggests to my mind a method of meeting the difficulty that you have just mentioned. Unless I am entirely mistaken, Miss Burnham will not say No to the change that I have in view for her.'

'What is it?' asked Mrs Crayford, eagerly.

'Pardon me if I ask you a question, on my part, before I reply,' said the doctor. 'Are you fortunate enough to possess any interest at the Admiralty?'

'Certainly. My father is in the Secretary's office – and two of the Lords of the Admiralty are friends of his.'

'Excellent! Now I can speak out plainly with little fear of disappointing you. After what I have said, you will agree with me that the only change in Miss Burnham's life which will be of any use to her, is a change that will alter the present tone of her mind on the subject of Mr Aldersley. Place her in a position to discover – not by reference to her own distempered fancies and visions, but by reference to actual evidence and actual fact – whether Mr Aldersley is, or is not, a living man; and there will be an end of the hysterical delusions which now threaten to fatally undermine her health. Even taking matters at their worst – even assuming that Mr Aldersley has died in the Arctic seas – it will be less injurious to her to discover this positively, than to leave her mind to feed on its own morbid superstitions and speculations, for weeks and weeks together, while the next news from the Expedition is on its way to England. In one word, I want you to be in a position, before the week is out, to put Miss Burnham's present convictions to a practical test. Suppose you could say to her: – "We differ, my dear, about Mr Francis Aldersley. You declare, without the shadow of a reason for it, that he is certainly dead, and, worse still, that he has died by the act of one of his brother officers. I assert, on the authority of the newspaper, that nothing of the sort has happened, and that the chances are all in favour of his being still a living man. What do you say to crossing the Atlantic, and deciding which of us is right – you or I?" Do you think Miss Burnham will say No to that, Mrs Crayford? If I know anything of human nature, she will seize the opportunity as a means of converting you to a belief in the Second Sight.'

'Good heavens, doctor! do you mean to tell me that we are to go out and meet the Arctic Expedition on its way home?'

'Admirably guessed, Mrs Crayford! That is exactly what I mean.'

'But how is it to be done?'

'I will tell you immediately. I mentioned – didn't I? – that I had heard something on my road to this house.'

'Yes?'

'Well, I met an old friend at my own gate, who walked with me a part of the way here. Last night my friend dined with the Admiral at Portsmouth. Among the guests there was a member of the Ministry, who had brought the news about the Expedition with him from London. This gentleman told the company there was very little doubt that the Admiralty would immediately send out a steam-vessel, to meet the rescued men on the shores of America, and bring them home. Wait a little, Mrs Crayford! Nobody knows, as yet, under what rules and regulations the vessel will sail. Under somewhat similar circumstances, privileged people *have* been received as passengers, or rather as guests, in Her Majesty's ships – and what has been conceded on former occasions may, by bare possibility, be conceded now. I can say no more. If you are not afraid of the voyage for yourself, I am not afraid of it (nay, I am all in favour of it on medical grounds) for my patient. What do you say? Will you write to your father, and ask him to try what his interest will do with his friends at the Admiralty?'

Mrs Crayford rose excitedly to her feet.

'Write!' she exclaimed. 'I will do better than write. The journey to London is no great matter – and my housekeeper here is to be trusted to take care of Clara in my absence. I will see my father to-night! He shall make good use of his interest at the Admiralty – you may rely on that. Oh, my dear doctor, what a prospect it is! My husband! Clara! What a discovery you have made – what a treasure you are! How can I thank you?'

'Compose yourself, my dear madam. Don't make too sure of success. We may consider Miss Burnham's objections as disposed of beforehand. But suppose the Lords of the Admiralty say No?'

'In that case I shall be in London, doctor; and I shall go to them myself. Lords are only men – and men are not in the habit of saying No to *me*.'

So they parted.

In a week from that day Her Majesty's ship *Amazon* sailed for North America. Certain privileged persons, specially interested in the Arctic voyagers, were permitted to occupy the empty state-rooms on board. On the list of these favoured guests of the ship were the names of two ladies – Mrs Crayford and Miss Burnham.

FIFTH SCENE

THE BOAT-HOUSE

CHAPTER XVI

Once more the open sea – the sea whose waters break on the shores of Newfoundland! An English steamship lies at anchor in the offing. The vessel is plainly visible through the open doorway of a large boat-house on the shore; one of the buildings attached to a fishing-station on the coast of the island.

The only person in the boat-house at this moment, is a man in the dress of a sailor. He is seated on a chest, with a piece of cord in his hand, looking out idly at the sea. On the rough carpenter's table near him lies a strange object to be left in such a place – a woman's veil.

What is the vessel lying at anchor in the offing?

The vessel is the *Amazon* – despatched from England to receive the surviving officers and men of the Arctic Expedition. The meeting has been successfully effected, on the shores of North America, three days since. But the homeward voyage has been delayed by a storm which has driven the ship out of her course. Taking advantage, on the third day, of the first returning calm, the commander of the *Amazon* has anchored off the coast of Newfoundland, and has sent ashore to increase his supplies of water before he sails for England. The weary passengers have landed for a few hours, to refresh themselves after the discomforts of the tempest. Among them are the two ladies. The veil left on the table in the boat-house is Clara's veil.

And who is the man sitting on the chest, with the cord in his hand, looking out idly at the sea? The man is the only cheerful person in the ship's company. In other words – John Want.

Still reposing on the chest, our friend who never grumbles, is surprised by the sudden appearance of a sailor at the boat-house door.

'Look sharp with your work, there, John Want!' says the sailor; 'Lieutenant Crayford is just coming to look after you.'

With this warning the messenger disappears again. John Want rises with a groan – turns the chest up on one end – and begins to fasten the cord round it. The ship's cook is not a man to look back on his rescue with the feeling of unmitigated satisfaction which animates his companions in trouble. On the contrary, he is ungratefully disposed to regret the North Pole.

'If I had only known' – thus runs the train of thought in the mind of John Want – if I had only known, before I was rescued, that I was to be brought to this place, I believe I should have preferred staying at the North Pole. I was very happy keeping up everbody's spirits at the North Pole. Taking one thing with another, I think I must have been very comfortable at the North Pole – if I had only known it. Another man in my place might be inclined to say that this Newfoundland boat-house was rather a sloppy, slimy, draughty, fishy sort of a habitation to take shelter in. Another man might object to perpetual Newfoundland fogs, perpetual Newfoundland codfish, and perpetual Newfoundland dogs. We had some very nice bears at the North Pole. Never mind! it's all one to me – I don't grumble.'

'Have you done cording that box?'

This time the voice is a voice of authority – the man at the doorway is Lieutenant Crayford himself. John Want answers his officer in his own cheerful way.

'I've done it as well as I can, sir – but the damp of this place is beginning to tell upon our very ropes. I say nothing about our lungs – I only say our ropes.'

Crayford answers sharply. He seems to have lost his former relish for the humour of John Want.

'Pooh! To look at your wry face, one would think that our rescue from the Arctic regions was a downright misfortune. You deserve to be sent back again.'

'I could be just as cheerful as ever, sir, if I *was* sent back again. I hope I'm thankful; but I don't like to hear the North Pole run down in such a fishy place as this. It was very clean and snowy at the North Pole – and it's very damp and sandy here. Do you never miss your bone soup, sir? *I* do. It mightn't have been strong; but it was very hot; and the cold seemed to give it a kind of a meaty flavour as it went down. Was it you that was a-coughing so long, last night, sir? I don't presume to say anything against the air of these latitudes – but I should be glad to know it wasn't you that was a-coughing so hollow. Would you be so obliging as just to feel the state of these ropes with the ends of your fingers, sir? You can dry them afterwards on the back of my jacket.'

'You ought to have a stick laid on the back of your jacket. Take that box down to the boat directly. You croaking vagabond! You would have grumbled in the Garden of Eden.'

The philosopher of the Expedition was not a man to be silenced by referring him to the Garden of Eden. Paradise itself was not perfect to John Want.

'I hope I could be cheerful anywhere, sir,' said the ship's cook. 'But you mark my words – there must have been a deal of troublesome work with the flower-beds in the Garden of Eden.'

Having entered that unanswerable protest, John Want shouldered the box, and drifted drearily out of the boat-house.

Left by himself, Crayford looked at his watch, and called to a sailor outside.

'Where are the ladies?' he asked.

'Mrs Crayford is coming this way, sir. She was just behind you when you came in.'

'Is Miss Burnham with her?'

'No, sir; Miss Burnham is down on the beach with the passengers. I heard the young lady asking after you, sir.'

'Asking after me?' Crayford considered with himself, as he repeated the words. He added, in lower and graver tones, 'You had better tell Miss Burnham you have seen me here.'

The man made his salute and went out. Crayford took a turn in the boat-house.

Rescued from death in the Arctic wastes, and reunited to a beautiful wife, the Lieutenant looked, nevertheless, unaccountably anxious and depressed. What could he be thinking of? He was thinking of Clara.

On the first day when the rescued men were received on board the *Amazon*, Clara had embarrassed and distressed, not Crayford only, but the other officers of the Expedition as well, by the manner in which she questioned them on the subject of Francis Aldersley and Richard Wardour. She had shown no signs of dismay or despair when she heard that no news had been received of the two missing men. She had even smiled sadly to herself, when Crayford (out of compassionate regard for her) declared that he and his comrades had not given up the hope of seeing Frank and Wardour yet. It was only when the Lieutenant had expressed himself in those terms – and when he had apparently succeeded in dismissing the painful subject – that Clara had startled every one present by announcing that she had something to say in relation to Richard and Frank, which had not been said yet. Though she spoke guardedly, her next words revealed suspicions of foul play lurking in her mind – exactly reflecting similar suspicions lurking in Crayford's mind – which so distressed the Lieutenant, and so surprised his comrades, as to render them quite incapable of answering her. The warnings of the storm which shortly afterwards broke over the vessel were then visible in sea and sky. Crayford made them his excuse for abruptly leaving the cabin in which the conversation had taken place. His brother officers, profiting by his example, pleaded their duties on deck, and followed him out.

On the next day, and the next, the tempest still raged, and the passengers were not able to leave their state-rooms. But now, when the weather had moderated and the ship had anchored – now, when officers and passengers alike were on shore, with leisure time at their disposal – Clara had opportunities of returning to the subject of the lost men, which would make it impossible for Crayford to plead an excuse for not answering her. How was he to meet those questions? How could he still keep her in ignorance of the truth?

These were the reflections which now troubled Crayford, and which presented him, after his rescue, in the strangely inappropriate character of a depressed and anxious man. His brother officers, as he well knew, looked to him to take the chief responsibility. If he declined to accept it, he would instantly confirm the horrible suspicion in Clara's mind. The emergency must be met; but how to meet it – at once honourably and mercifully – was more than Crayford could tell. He was still lost in his own gloomy thoughts, when his wife entered the boat-house. Turning to look at her, he saw his own perturbations and anxieties plainly reflected in Mrs Crayford's face.

'Have you seen anything of Clara?' he asked. 'Is she still on the beach?'

'She is following me to this place,' Mrs Crayford replied. 'I have been speaking to her this morning. She is just as resolute as ever to insist on your telling her of the circumstances under which Frank is missing. As things are, you have no alternative but to answer her.'

'Help me to answer her, Lucy. Tell me, before she comes in, how this horrible suspicion first took possession of her. All she could possibly have known, when we left England, was that the two men were appointed to separate ships. What could have led her to suspect that they had come together?'

'She was firmly persuaded, William, that they *would* come together, when the Expedition left England. And she had read in books of Arctic travel, of men left behind by their comrades on the march, and of men adrift on icebergs. With her mind full of these images and forebodings, she saw Frank and Wardour (or dreamed of them) in one of her attacks of trance. I was by her side – I heard what she said at the time. She warned Frank that Wardour had discovered the truth. She called out to him, "While you can stand, keep with the other men, Frank!——"

'Good God!' cried Crayford; 'I warned him myself, almost in those very words, the last time I saw him.'

'Don't acknowledge it, William! Keep her in ignorance of what you have just told me; she will not take it for what it is – a startling coincidence, and nothing more. She will accept it as positive confirmation of the faith, the miserable superstitious faith, that is in her. So long as you don't actually know that Frank is dead, and that he has

died by Wardour's hand, deny what she says – mislead her for her own
sake – dispute all her conclusions as I dispute them. Help me to raise her
to the better and nobler belief in the mercy of God!' She stopped and
looked round nervously at the doorway. 'Hush!' she whispered; 'do as I
have told you. Clara is here.'

CHAPTER XVII

Clara stopped at the doorway, looking backwards and forwards
distrustfully between the husband and wife. Entering the boat-house, and
approaching Crayford, she took his arm and led him away a few steps
from the place in which Mrs Crayford was standing.

'There is no storm now, and there are no duties to be done on board
the ship,' she said, with a faint sad smile which it wrung Crayford's heart
to see. 'You are Lucy's husband, and you have an interest in me for Lucy's
sake. Don't shrink on that account from giving me pain: I can bear pain.
Friend and brother, will you believe that I have courage enough to hear
the worst? Will you promise not to deceive me about Frank?'

The gentle resignation in her voice, the sad pleading in her look,
shook Crayford's self-possession at the outset. He answered her in the
worst possible manner – he answered evasively.

'My dear Clara,' he said, 'what have I done that you should suspect me
of deceiving you?'

She looked him searchingly in the face – then glanced with renewed
distrust at Mrs Crayford. There was a moment of silence. Before any of
the three could speak again, they were interrupted by the appearance of
one of Crayford's brother officers, followed by two sailors carrying a
hamper between them. Crayford instantly dropped Clara's arm, and
seized the welcome opportunity of speaking of other things.

'Any instructions from the ship, Steventon?' he asked, approaching the
officer.

'Verbal instructions only,' Steventon replied. 'The ship will sail with the
flood tide. We shall fire a gun to collect the people, and send another
boat ashore. In the meantime here are some refreshments for the
passengers. The vessel is in a state of confusion; the ladies will eat their
lunch more comfortably here.'

Hearing this, Mrs Crayford took *her* opportunity of silencing Clara next.

'Come, my dear,' she said, 'let us lay the cloth and put the lunch on the
table before the gentlemen come in.'

Clara was too seriously bent on attaining the object which she had in
view, to be silenced in that way. 'I will help you directly,' she answered –

then crossed the room and addressed herself to the officer whose name was Steventon.

'Can you spare me a few minutes?' she asked; 'I have something to say to you.'

'I am entirely at your service, Miss Burnham.'

Answering in those words, Steventon dismissed the two sailors. Mrs Crayford looked anxiously at her husband. Crayford whispered to her, 'Don't be alarmed about Steventon. I have cautioned him; I believe he is to be depended on.'

Clara beckoned to Crayford to return to her.

'I will not keep you long,' she said; 'I will promise not to distress Mr Steventon. Young as I am, you shall both find that I am capable of self-control. I won't ask you to go back to the story of your past sufferings; I only want to be sure that I am right about one thing – I mean about what happened at the time when the exploring party was despatched in search of help. As I understand it, you cast lots among yourselves who was to go with the party, and who was to remain behind. Frank cast the lot to go.' She paused, shuddering. 'And Richard Wardour,' she went on, 'cast the lot to remain behind. On your honour, as officers and gentlemen, is this the truth?'

'On my honour,' Crayford answered, 'it is the truth.'

'On my honour,' Steventon repeated, 'it is the truth.'

She looked at them, carefully considering her next words before she spoke again.

'You both drew the lot to stay in the huts,' she said, addressing Crayford and Steventon, 'and you are both here. Richard Wardour drew the lot to stay, and Richard Wardour is not here. How does his name come to be with Frank's on the list of the missing?'

The question was a dangerous one to answer. Steventon left it to Crayford to reply. Once again he answered evasively.

'It doesn't follow, my dear,' he said, 'that the two men were missing together, because their names happen to come together on the list.'

Clara instantly drew the inevitable conclusion from that ill-considered reply.

'Frank is missing from the party of relief,' she said. 'Am I to understand that Wardour is missing from the huts?'

Both Crayford and Steventon hesitated. Mrs Crayford cast one indignant look at them, and told the necessary lie without a moment's hesitation!

'Yes!' she said. 'Wardour is missing from the huts.'

Quickly as she had spoken, she had still spoken too late. Clara had noticed the momentary hesitation on the part of the two officers. She turned to Steventon.

'I trust to your honour,' she said, quietly. 'Am I right, or wrong, in believing that Mrs Crayford is mistaken?'

She had addressed herself to the right man of the two. Steventon had no wife present to exercise authority over him. Steventon, put on his honour and fairly forced to say something, owned the truth. Wardour had replaced an officer whom accident had disabled from accompanying the party of relief, and Wardour and Frank were missing together.

Clara looked at Mrs Crayford.

'You hear?' she said. 'It is you who are mistaken; not I. What you call "accident" – what I call "fate" – brought Richard Wardour and Frank together as members of the same Expedition after all.' Without waiting for a reply, she again turned to Steventon and surprised him by changing the painful subject of the conversation of her own accord.

'Have you been in the Highlands of Scotland?' she asked.

'I have never been in the Highlands,' Steventon replied.

'Have you ever read, in books about the Highlands, of such a thing as "The Second Sight?"'

'Yes.'

'Do you believe in the Second Sight?'

Steventon politely declined to commit himself to a direct reply.

'I don't know what I might have done if I had ever been in the Highlands,' he said. 'As it is, I have had no opportunities of giving the subject any serious consideration.'

'I won't put your credulity to the test,' Clara proceeded. 'I won't ask you to believe anything more extraordinary than that I had a strange dream in England not very long since. My dream showed me what you have just acknowledged – and more than that. How did the two missing men come to be parted from their companions? Were they lost by pure accident? or were they deliberately left behind on the march?'

Crayford made a last vain effort to check her enquiries at the point which they had now reached.

'Neither Steventon nor I were members of the party of relief,' he said. 'How are we to answer you?'

'Your brother officers who *were* members of the party must have told you what happened,' Clara rejoined. 'I only ask you and Mr Steventon to tell me what they told you.'

Mrs Crayford interposed again – with a practical suggestion this time.

'The luncheon is not unpacked yet,' she said. 'Come, Clara! this is our business, and the time is passing.'

'The luncheon can wait a few minutes longer,' Clara answered. 'Bear with my obstinacy,' she went on, laying her hand caressingly on Crayford's shoulder. 'Tell me how those two came to be separated from the rest. You have always been the kindest of friends; don't begin to be cruel to me now!'

The tone in which she made her entreaty to Crayford went straight to the sailor's heart. He gave up the hopeless struggle; he let her see a glimpse of the truth.

'On the third day out,' he said, 'Frank's strength failed him. He fell behind the rest from fatigue.'

'Surely they waited for him?'

'It was a serious risk to wait for him, my child. Their lives, and the lives of the men they had left in the huts, depended, in that dreadful climate, on their pushing on. But Frank was a favourite. They waited half a day to give Frank the chance of recovering his strength.'

There he stopped. There the imprudence into which his fondness for Clara had led him showed itself plainly, and closed his lips.

It was too late to take refuge in silence. Clara was determined on hearing more.

She questioned Steventon next.

'Did Frank go on again after the half-day's rest?' she asked.

'He tried to go on——'

'And failed?'

'Yes.'

'What did the men do when he failed? Did they turn cowards? Did they desert Frank?'

She had purposely used language which might irritate Steventon into answering her plainly. He was a young man; he fell into the snare that she had set for him.

'Not one among them was a coward, Miss Burnham!' he replied, warmly. 'You are speaking cruelly and unjustly of as brave a set of fellows as ever lived. The strongest man among them set the example: he volunteered to stay by Frank and to bring him on in the track of the exploring party.'

There Steventon stopped, conscious, on his side, that he had said too much. Would she ask him who this volunteer was? No. She went straight on to the most embarrassing question that she had put yet – referring to the volunteer, as if Steventon had already mentioned his name.

'What made Richard Wardour so ready to risk his life for Frank's sake?' she said to Crayford. 'Did he do it out of friendship for Frank? Surely you can tell me that? Carry your memory back to the days when you were all living in the huts. Were Frank and Wardour friends at that time? Did you never hear any angry words pass between them?'

There Mrs Crayford saw her opportunity of giving her husband a timely hint.

'My dear child!' she said. 'How can you expect him to remember that? There must have been plenty of quarrels among the men, all shut up together, and all weary of each other's company, no doubt.'

'Plenty of quarrels!' Crayford repeated – 'and every one of them made up again.'

'And every one of them made up again,' Mrs Crayford reiterated, in her turn. 'There! a plainer answer than that you can't wish to have. *Now* are you satisfied? Mr Steventon, come and lend a hand (as you say at sea) with the hamper – Clara won't help me. William! Don't stand there doing nothing. This hamper holds a great deal; we must have a division of labour. Your division shall be laying the tablecloth. Don't handle it in that clumsy way! You unfold a tablecloth as if you were unfurling a sail. Put the knives on the right, and the forks on the left, and the napkin and bread between them. Clara! if you are not hungry in this fine air, you ought to be. Come and do your duty – come and have some lunch!'

She looked up as she spoke. Clara appeared to have yielded at last to the conspiracy to keep her in the dark. She had returned slowly to the boat-house doorway; and she was standing alone on the threshold, looking out. Approaching her to lead her to the luncheon-table, Mrs Crayford could hear that she was speaking softly to herself. She was repeating the farewell words which Richard Wardour had spoken to her at the ball.

'"A time may come when I shall forgive *you*. But the man who has robbed me of you shall rue the day when you and he first met." Oh, Frank! Frank! does Richard still live – with your blood on his conscience, and my image in his heart?'

Her lips suddenly closed. She started, and drew back from the doorway, trembling violently. Mrs Crayford looked out at the quiet seaward view.

'Anything there that frightens you, my dear?' she asked. 'I can see nothing – except the boats drawn up on the beach.'

'*I* can see nothing either, Lucy.'

'And yet, you are trembling as if there was something dreadful in the view from this door.'

'There *is* something dreadful! I feel it – though I see nothing. I feel it – nearer and nearer in the empty air, darker and darker in the sunny light. I don't know what it is. Take me away! No. Not out on the beach. I can't pass the door. Somewhere else! somewhere else!'

Mrs Crayford looked round her, and noticed a second door at the inner end of the boat-house. She spoke to her husband.

'See where that door leads to, William.'

Crayford opened the door. It led into a desolate enclosure – half garden, half yard. Some nets, stretched on poles, were hanging up to dry. No other objects were visible – not a living creature appeared in the place. 'It doesn't look very inviting, my dear,' said Mrs Crayford. 'I am at your service, however. What do you say?'

She offered her arm to Clara as she spoke. Clara refused it. She took Crayford's arm, and clung to him.

'I'm frightened, dreadfully frightened!' she said to him, faintly. '*You* keep with me – a woman is no protection; I want to be with *you*.' She looked round again at the boat-house doorway. 'Oh!' she whispered, 'I'm cold all over – I'm frozen with fear of this place. Come into the yard! Come into the yard!'

'Leave her to me,' said Crayford to his wife. 'I will call you, if she doesn't get better in the open air.'

He took her out at once, and closed the yard door behind them.

'Mr Steventon! do you understand this?' asked Mrs Crayford. 'What can she possibly be frightened of?'

She put the question, still looking mechanically at the door by which her husband and Clara had gone out. Receiving no reply, she glanced round at Steventon. He was standing on the opposite side of the luncheon-table, with his eyes fixed attentively on the view from the main doorway of the boat-house. Mrs Crayford looked where Steventon was looking. This time, there was something visible. She saw the shadow of a human figure projected on the stretch of smooth yellow sand in front of the boat-house.

In a moment more, the figure appeared. A man came slowly into view and stopped on the threshold of the door.

CHAPTER XVIII

The man was a sinister and terrible object to look at. His eyes glared like the eyes of a wild animal; his head was bare; his long grey hair was torn and tangled; his miserable garments hung about him in rags. He stood in the doorway, a speechless figure of misery and want, staring at the well-spread table like a hungry dog.

Steventon spoke to him.

'Who are you?'

He answered in a hollow voice:

'A starving man.'

He advanced a few steps – slowly and painfully, as if he was sinking under fatigue.

'Throw me some bones from the table,' he said. 'Give me my share along with the dogs.'

There was madness as well as hunger in his eyes while he spoke these words. Steventon placed Mrs Crayford behind him, so that he might be easily able to protect her in case of need, and beckoned to two sailors who were passing the door of the boat-house at the time.

'Give the man some bread and meat,' he said, 'and wait near him.'

The outcast seized on the bread and meat with lean, long-nailed hands that looked like claws. After the first mouthful of food, he stopped, considered vacantly with himself, and broke the bread and meat into two portions. One portion he put into an old canvas wallet that hung over his shoulder. The other he devoured voraciously. Steventon questioned him.

'Where do you come from?'

'From the sea.'

'Wrecked?'

'Yes.'

Steventon turned to Mrs Crayford.

'There may be some truth in the poor wretch's story,' he said. 'I heard something of a strange boat having been cast on the beach, thirty or forty miles higher up the coast. When were you wrecked, my man?'

The starving creature looked up from his food, and made an effort to collect his thoughts – to exert his memory. It was not to be done. He gave up the attempt in despair. His language, when he spoke, was as wild as his looks.

'I can't tell you,' he said. 'I can't get the wash of the sea out of my ears. I can't get the shining stars all night, and the burning sun all day, out of my brain. When was I wrecked? When was I first adrift in the boat? When did I get the tiller in my hand and fight against hunger and sleep? When did the gnawing in my breast, and the burning in my head, first begin? I have lost all reckoning of it. I can't think; I can't sleep; I can't get the wash of the sea out of my ears. What are you baiting me with questions for? Let me eat!'

Even the sailors pitied him. The sailors asked leave of their officer to add a little drink to his meal.

'We've got a drop of grog with us, sir, in a bottle. May we give it to him?'

'Certainly!'

He took the bottle fiercely, as he had taken the food – drank a little – stopped – and considered with himself again. He held up the bottle to the light, and, marking how much liquor it contained, carefully drank half of it only. This done, he put the bottle in his wallet along with the food.

'Are you saving it up for another time?' said Steventon.

'I'm saving it up,' the man answered. 'Never mind what for. That's my secret.'

He looked round the boat-house as he made that reply, and noticed Mrs Crayford for the first time.

'A woman among you!' he said. 'Is she English? Is she young? Let me look closer at her.'

He advanced a few steps towards the table.

'Don't be afraid, Mrs Crayford,' said Steventon.

'I'm not afraid,' Mrs Crayford replied. 'He frightened me at first – he interests me now. Let him speak to me if he wishes it.'

He never spoke. He stood, in dead silence, looking long and anxiously at the beautiful Englishwoman.

'Well?' said Steventon.

He shook his head sadly, and drew back again with a heavy sigh.

'No!' he said to himself, 'that's not *her* face. No! not found yet.'

Mrs Crayford's interest was strongly excited. She ventured to speak to him.

'Who is it you want to find?' she asked. 'Your wife?'

He shook his head again.

'Who then? What is she like?'

He answered that question in words. His hoarse, hollow voice softened little by little into sorrowful and gentle tones.

'Young,' he said; 'with a fair, sad face – with kind, tender eyes – with a soft, clear voice. Young, and loving, and merciful. I keep her face in my mind, though I can keep nothing else. I must wander, wander, wander – restless, sleepless, homeless – till I find *her*! Over the ice and over the snow; tossing on the sea, tramping over the land; awake all night, awake all day; wander, wander, wander, till I find *her*!'

He waved his hand with a gesture of farewell, and turned wearily to go out.

At the same moment Crayford opened the yard door.

'I think you had better come to Clara,' he began – and checked himself, noticing the stranger. 'Who is that?'

The shipwrecked man, hearing another voice in the room, looked round slowly over his shoulder. Struck by his appearance, Crayford advanced a little nearer to him. Mrs Crayford spoke to her husband as he passed her.

'It's only a poor mad creature, William,' she whispered, 'shipwrecked and starving.'

'Mad?' Crayford repeated, approaching nearer and nearer to the man. 'Am *I* in my right senses?' He suddenly sprang on the outcast, and seized him by the throat. 'Richard Wardour!' he cried, in a voice of fury. 'Alive! Alive, to answer for Frank!'

The man struggled. Crayford held him.

'Where is Frank?' he said. 'You villain, where is Frank?'

The man resisted no longer. He repeated vacantly –

'Villain? and where is Frank?'

As the name escaped his lips, Clara appeared at the open yard door, and hurried into the room.

'I heard Richard Wardour's name!' she said. 'I heard Frank's name! What does it mean?'

At the sound of her voice the outcast renewed the struggle to free himself, with a sudden frenzy of strength which Crayford was not able to resist. He broke away before the sailors could come to their officer's assistance. Half way down the length of the room he and Clara met one another face to face. A new light sparkled in the poor wretch's eyes; a cry of recognition burst from his lips. He flung one hand up wildly in the air. 'Found!' he shouted, and rushed out to the beach before any of the men present could stop him.

Mrs Crayford put her arms round Clara and held her up. She had not made a movement; she had not spoken a word. The sight of Wardour's face had petrified her.

The minutes passed, and there rose a sudden burst of cheering from the sailors on the beach, near the spot where the fishermen's boats were drawn up. Every man left his work. Every man waved his cap in the air. The passengers, near at hand, caught the infection of enthusiasm, and joined the crew. A moment more, and Richard Wardour appeared again in the doorway, carrying a man in his arms. He staggered, breathless with the effort that he was making, to the place where Clara stood, held up in Mrs Crayford's arms.

'Saved, Clara!' he cried. 'Saved for *you!*'

He released the man, and placed him in Clara's arms.

Frank! Footsore and weary, but living! Saved – saved for *her!* 'Now, Clara,' cried Mrs Crayford, 'which of us is right? I who believed in the mercy of God, or you who believed in a dream?'

She never answered; she clung to Frank in speechless ecstasy. She never even looked at the man who had preserved him – in the first absorbing joy of seeing her lover alive. Step by step, slower and slower, Richard Wardour drew back and left them by themselves.

'I may rest now,' he said, faintly. 'I may sleep at last. The task is done. The struggle is over.'

His last reserves of strength had been given to Frank. He stopped, he staggered, his hands wavered feebly in search of support. But for one faithful friend, he would have fallen. Crayford caught him. Crayford laid his old comrade gently on some sails strewn in a corner, and pillowed Wardour's weary head on his own breast. The tears streamed over his face. 'Richard! Dear Richard!' he said. 'Remember – and forgive me.'

Richard neither heeded nor heard him. His dim eyes still looked across the room at Clara and Frank.

'I have made *her* happy!' he murmured. 'I may lay down my weary head now on the mother earth that hushes all her children to rest at last. Sink, heart! sink, sink to rest! Oh, look at them!' he said to Crayford, with a burst of grief. 'They have forgotten *me* already.'

It was true! The interest was all with the two lovers. Frank was young, and handsome, and popular. Officers, passengers, and sailors, they all crowded round Frank. They all forgot the martyred man who had saved him – the man who was dying in Crayford's arms.

Crayford tried once more to attract his attention – to win his recognition while there was yet time.

'Richard, speak to me! Speak to your old friend!'

He looked round; he vacantly repeated Crayford's last word.

'Friend?' he said. 'My eyes are dim, friend; my mind is dull. I have lost all memories but the memory of *her*. Dead thoughts – all dead thoughts but that one! And yet, you look at me kindly! Why has your face gone down with the wreck of all the rest?'

He paused. His face changed; his thoughts drifted back from present to past. He looked at Crayford vacantly, lost in the terrible remembrances that were rising in him, as the shadows rise with the coming night.

'Hark ye, friend!' he whispered. 'Never let Frank know it. There was a time when the fiend within me hungered for his life. I had my hands on the boat. I heard the voice of the Tempter speaking to me: "Launch it, and leave him to die!" I waited, with my hands on the boat and my eyes on the place where he slept. "Leave him, leave him!" the Voice whispered. "Love him!" the lad's voice answered, moaning and murmuring in his sleep. "Love him, Clara, for helping *me!*" I heard the morning wind come up in the silence over the great deep. Far and near, I heard the groaning of the floating ice, floating, floating, to the clear water and the balmy air. And the wicked Voice floated away with it – away, away, away for ever! "Love him! love him, Clara, for helping *me*." No wind could float that away. "Love him, Clara"——'

His voice sank into silence; his head dropped on Crayford's breast. Frank saw it. Frank struggled up on his bleeding feet, and parted the friendly throng round him. Frank had not forgotten the man who had saved him.

'Let me go to him!' he cried. 'I must, and will, go to him! Clara, come with me.'

Clara and Steventon supported him between them. He fell on his knees at Wardour's side; he put his head on Wardour's bosom.

'Richard!'

The weary eyes opened again. The sinking voice was heard feebly once more.

'Ah! poor Frank. I didn't forget you, Frank, when I came here to beg. I remembered you, lying down outside in the shadow of the boats. I saved you your share of the food and drink. Too weak to get at it now! A little rest, Frank! I shall soon be strong enough to carry you down to the ship.'

The end was near. They all saw it now. The men reverently uncovered their heads in the presence of Death. In an agony of despair, Frank appealed to the friends round him.

'Get something to strengthen him, for God's sake! Oh, men! men! I should never have been here but for him! He has given all his strength to my weakness; and now, see how strong I am, and how weak *he* is! Clara! I held by his arm all over the ice and snow. *He* kept watch when I was senseless in the open boat. *His* hand dragged me out of the waves, when we were wrecked. Speak to him, Clara! speak to him!' His voice failed him, and his head dropped on Wardour's breast.

She spoke, as well as her tears would let her.

'Richard! have you forgotten me?'

He rallied at the sound of that beloved voice. He looked up at her, as she knelt at his head.

'Forgotten you?' Still looking at her, he lifted his hand with an effort, and laid it on Frank. 'Should I have been strong enough to save *him*, if I could have forgotten *you*?' He waited a moment, and turned his head feebly towards Crayford. 'Stay!' he said. 'Some one was here and spoke to me!' A faint light of recognition glimmered in his eyes. 'Ah, Crayford! I recollect now. Dear Crayford! Come nearer! My mind clears; but my eyes grow dim. You will remember me kindly for Frank's sake? Poor Frank! why does he hide his face? Is he crying? Nearer, Clara – I want to look my last at *you*. My sister Clara! Kiss me, sister, kiss me before I die!'

She stooped and kissed his forehead. A faint smile trembled on his lips. It passed away; and stillness possessed the face – the stillness of Death.

Crayford's voice was heard in the silence.

'The loss is ours,' he said. 'The gain is his. He has won the greatest of all conquests – the conquest of himself. And he has died in the moment of victory. Not one of us here but may live to envy *his* glorious death.'

The distant report of a gun came from the ship in the offing, and signalled the return to England and to home.

MR WRAY'S CASH-BOX

INTRODUCTION

It may possibly happen that some of the readers of this story have in their possession a plaster 'mask' – or, face and forehead – of Shakspeare, which is a cast from the celebrated Stratford bust. These casts were first offered for sale not very long since. The circumstances under which the original mould was taken, I heard thus related by a friend (now no more), to whose affectionate remembrance of me I am indebted for the specimen of the mask which I now possess.

A stone-mason at Stratford-upon-Avon was employed, a few years ago, to make repairs in the church. While thus engaged, he managed – as he thought, unsuspected – to take a mould from the Shakspeare bust. What he had done was found out, however; and he was forthwith threatened, by the authorities having care of the bust, with the severest pains and penalties of the law – though for what special offence was not specified. The poor man was so frightened at these menaces, that he packed up his tools at once, and, taking the mould with him, left Stratford. Having afterwards stated his case to persons competent to advise him, he was told that he need fear no penalty whatever, and that if he thought he could dispose of them, he might make as many casts as he pleased, and offer them for sale anywhere. He took the advice, placed his masks neatly on slabs of black marble, and sold great numbers of them, not only in England, but in America also. It should be added, that this stone-mason had been always remarkable for his extraordinary reverence of Shakspeare, which he carried to such an extent, as to assure the friend from whom I derived the information here given, that if (as a widower) he ever married again, it should be only when he could meet with a woman who was a lineal descendant of William Shakspeare!

From the anecdote I have related, the first idea of the following pages was derived. I now offer my little book to the public, strictly for what it is called on the title page – a 'sketch;' in writing which I have endeavoured to tell a simple story, simply and familiarly; or, in other words, as if I were only telling it to an audience of friends at my own fireside.

W.W. COLLINS

HANOVER TERRACE, REGENT'S PARK:
December, 1851.

CHAPTER I

ELOCUTION FOR THE MILLION

I should be insulting the intelligence of readers generally, if I thought it at all necessary to describe to them that widely-celebrated town, Tidbury-on-the-Marsh. As a genteel provincial residence, who is unacquainted with it? The magnificent new Hotel that has grown on to the side of the old Inn; the extensive Library, to which, not satisfied with only adding new books, they are now adding a new entrance as well; the projected Crescent of palatial abodes in the Grecian style, on the top of the hill, to rival the completed Crescent of castellated abodes, in the Gothic style, at the bottom of the hill – are not such local objects as these perfectly well known to any intelligent Englishman? Of course they are! The question is superfluous. Let us get on at once, without wasting more time, from Tidbury in general to the High Street in particular, and to our present destination there – the commercial establishment of Messrs. Dunball and Dark.

Looking merely at the coloured liquids, the miniature statue of a horse, the corn-plasters, the oil-skin bags, the pots of cosmetics, and the cut-glass saucers full of lozenges in the shop-window, you might at first imagine that Dunball and Dark were only chemists. Looking carefully through the entrance, towards an inner apartment, an inscription; a large, upright, mahogany receptacle, or box, with a hole in it; brass rails protecting the hole; a green curtain ready to draw over the hole; and a man with a copper money-shovel in his hand, partially visible behind the hole; would be sufficient to inform you that Dunball and Dark were not chemists only, but 'Branch Bankers' as well.

It is a rough squally morning at the end of November. Mr Dunball (in the absence of Mr Dark, who has gone to make a speech at the Vestry Meeting) has got into the mahogany box, and has assumed the whole business and direction of the Branch Bank. He is a very fat man, and looks absurdly over large for his sphere of action. Not a single customer has, as yet, applied for money – nobody has come even to gossip with the Branch Banker through the brass rails of his commercial prison-house. There he sits, staring calmly through the chemical part of the shop into the street – his gold in one drawer, his notes in another, his elbows on his ledgers, his copper shovel under his thumb; the picture of monied loneliness; the hermit of British finances.

In the outer shop is the young assistant, ready to drug the public at a moment's notice. But Tidbury-on-the-Marsh is an unprofitably healthy place; and no public appears. By the time the young assistant has ascertained from the shop clock that it is a quarter past ten, and from the weather-cock opposite that the wind is 'Sou'-sou'-west,' he has exhausted all external sources of amusement, and is reduced to occupying himself by first sharpening his penknife, and then cutting his nails. He has completed his left hand, and has just begun on the right hand thumb, when a customer actually darkens the shop-door at last!

Mr Dunball starts, and grasps the copper shovel: the young assistant shuts up his pen-knife in a hurry, and makes a bow. The customer is a young girl, and she has come for a pot of lip-salve.

She is very neatly and quietly dressed; looks about eighteen or nineteen years of age; and has something in her face which I can only characterise by the epithet – loveable. There is a beauty of innocence and purity about her forehead, brow, and eyes – a calm, kind, happy expression as she looks at you – and a curious home-sound in her clear utterance when she speaks, which, altogether, make you fancy, stranger as you are, that you must have known her and loved her long ago, and somehow or other ungratefully forgotten her in the lapse of time. Mixed up, however, with the girlish gentleness and innocence which form her more prominent charm, there is a look of firmness – especially noticeable about the expression of her lips – that gives a certain character and originality to her face. Her figure——

I stop at her figure. Not by any means for want of phrases to describe it; but from a disheartening conviction of the powerlessness of any description of her at all to produce the right effect on the minds of others. If I were asked in what particular efforts of literature the poverty of literary material most remarkably appears, I should answer, in personal descriptions of heroines. We have all read these by the hundred – some of them so carefully and finely finished, that we are not only informed about the lady's eyes, eyebrows, nose, cheeks, complexion, mouth, teeth, neck, ears, head, hair, and the way it was dressed; but are also made acquainted with the particular manner in which the sentiments below made the bosom above heave or swell; besides the exact position of head in which her eyelashes were just long enough to cast a shadow on her cheeks. We have read all this attentively and admiringly, as it deserves; and have yet risen from the reading, without the remotest approach to a realization in our own minds of what sort of a woman the heroine really was. We vaguely knew she was beautiful, at the beginning of the description; and we know just as much – just as vaguely – at the end.

Penetrated with the conviction above-mentioned, I prefer leaving the reader to form his own realisation of the personal appearance of the customer at Messrs. Dunball and Dark's. Eschewing the magnificent beauties of his acquaintance, let him imagine her to be like any pretty intelligent girl whom he knows – any of those pleasant little fire-side angels, who can charm us even in a merino morning gown, darning an old pair of socks. Let this be the sort of female reality in the reader's mind; and neither author, nor heroine, need have any reason to complain.

Well; our young lady came to the counter, and asked for lip-salve. The assistant, vanquished at once by the potent charm of her presence, paid her the first little tribute of politeness in his power, by asking permission to send the gallipot home for her.

'I beg your pardon, miss,' said he; 'but I think you live lower down, at No. 12. I was passing; and I think I saw you going in there, yesterday, with an old gentleman, and another gentleman – I think I did, miss?'

'Yes: we lodge at No. 12,' said the young girl; 'but I will take the lip-salve home with me, if you please. I have a favour, however, to ask of you before I go,' she continued very modestly, but without the slightest appearance of embarrassment; 'if you have room to hang this up in your window, my grandfather, Mr Wray, would feel much obliged by your kindness.'

And here, to the utter astonishment of the young assistant, she handed him a piece of card-board, with a string to hang it up by, on which appeared the following inscription, neatly written:–

Mr Reuben Wray, pupil of the late celebrated John Kemble, Esquire, begs respectfully to inform his friends and the public that he gives lessons in elocution, delivery, and reading aloud, price two-and-sixpence the lesson of an hour. Pupils prepared for the stage, or private theatricals, on a principle combining intelligent interpretation of the text, with the action of the arms and legs adopted by the late illustrious Roscius of the English stage, J. Kemble, Esquire; and attentively studied from close observation of Mr J.K. by Mr R.W. Orators and clergymen improved (with the strictest secresy), at three-and-sixpence the lesson of an hour. Impediments and hesitation of utterance combated and removed. Young ladies taught the graces of delivery, and young gentlemen the proprieties of diction. A discount allowed to schools and large classes. Please to address, Mr Reuben Wray (late of the Theatre Royal, Drury Lane), 12, High-street, Tidbury-on-the-Marsh.

No Babylonian inscription that ever was cut, no manuscript on papyrus that ever was penned, could possibly have puzzled the young assistant more than this remarkable advertisement. He read it all through in a state of stupefaction; and then observed, with a bewildered look at the young girl on the other side of the counter;–

'Very nicely written, miss; and very nicely composed indeed! I suppose – in fact, I'm sure Mr Dunball' – Here a creaking was heard, as of some strong wooden construction being gradually rent asunder. It was Mr Dunball himself, squeezing his way out of the Branch Bank box, and coming to examine the advertisement.

He read it all through very attentively, following each line with his forefinger; and then cautiously and gently laid the card-board down on the counter. When I state that neither Mr Dunball nor his assistant were quite certain what a 'Roscius of the English stage' meant, or what precise branch of human attainment Mr Wray designed to teach in teaching 'Elocution,' I do no injustice either to master or man.

'So you want this hung up in the window, my – in the window, miss?' asked Mr Dunball. He was about to say, 'my dear;' but something in the girl's look and manner stopped him.

'If you could hang it up without inconvenience, sir.'

'May I ask what's your name? and where you come from?'

'My name is Annie Wray; and the last place we came from was Stratford-upon-Avon.'

'Ah! indeed – and Mr Wray teaches, does he? – elocution for half-a-crown – eh?'

'My grandfather only desires to let the inhabitant of this place know that he can teach those who wish it, to speak or read with a good delivery and a proper pronunciation.'

Mr Dunball felt rather puzzled by the straight-forward, self-possessed manner in which he – a branch banker, a chemist, and a municipal authority – was answered by little Annie Wray. He took up the advertisement again; and walked away to read it a second time in the solemn monetary seclusion of the back shop.

The young assistant followed. 'I think they're respectable people, sir,' said he, in a whisper; 'I was passing when the old gentleman went into No. 12, yesterday. The wind blew his cloak on one side, and I saw him carrying a large cash-box under it – I did indeed, sir; and it seemed a heavy one.'

'Cash-box!' cried Mr Dunball. 'What does a man with a cash-box want with elocution, and two-and-sixpence an hour?' Suppose he should be a swindler!'

'He can't be, sir: look at the young lady! Besides, the people at No. 12 told me he gave a reference, and paid a week's rent in advance.'

'He did – did he? I say, are you sure it was a cash-box?'

'Certain, sir. I suppose it had money in it, of course?'

'What's the use of a cash-box, without cash?' said the Branch Banker, contemptuously. 'It looks rather odd, though! Stop! maybe it's a wager.

I've heard of gentlemen doing queer things for wagers. Or, maybe, he's cracked! Well, she's a nice girl; and hanging up this thing can't do any harm. I'll make inquiries about them, though, for all that.'

Frowning portentously as he uttered this last cautious resolve, Mr Dunball leisurely returned into the chemist's shop. He was, however, nothing like so ill-natured a man as he imagined himself to be; and, in spite of his dignity and his suspicions, he smiled far more cordially than he at all intended, as he now addressed little Annie Wray.

'It's out of our line, miss,' said he; 'but we'll hang the thing up to oblige you. Of course, if I want a reference, you can give it? Yes, yes! of course. There! there's the card in the window for you – a nice prominent place (look at it as you go out) – just between the string of corn-plasters and the dried poppy-heads! I wish Mr Wray success; though I rather think Tidbury is not quite the sort of place to come to for what you call elocution – eh?'

'Thank you, sir; and good morning,' said little Annie. And she left the shop just as composedly as she had entered it.

'Cool little girl, that!' said Mr Dunball, watching her progress down the street to No. 12.

'Pretty little girl, too!' thought the assistant, trying to watch, like his master, from the window.

'I should like to know who Mr Wray is,' said Mr Dunball, turning back into the shop, as Annie disappeared. 'And I'd give something to find out what Mr Wray keeps in his cash-box,' continued the banker-chemist, as he thoughtfully re-entered the mahogany money-chest in the back premises.

You are a wise man, Mr Dunball; but you won't solve those two mysteries in a hurry, sitting alone in that Branch Bank sentry-box of yours! – Can anybody solve them? I can.

Who is Mr Wray? and what has he got in his cash-box? – Come to No. 12, and see!

CHAPTER II

MR WRAY AND THE BRITISH DRAMA

Before we go boldly into Mr Wray's lodgings, I must first speak a word or two about him, behind his back – but by no means slanderously. I will take his advertisement, now hanging up in the shop window of Messrs. Dunball and Dark, as the text of my discourse.

Mr Reuben Wray became, as he phrased it, a 'pupil of the late celebrated John Kemble, Esquire,' in this manner. He began life by being apprenticed for three years to a statuary. Whether the occupation of taking casts and clipping stones proved of too sedentary a nature to suit his temperament, or whether an evil counsellor within him, whose name was VANITY, whispered:– 'Seek public admiration, and be certain of public applause,' – I know not; but the fact is, that, as soon as his time was out, he left his master and his native place to join a company of strolling players; or, as he himself more magniloquently expressed it, he went on the stage.

Nature had gifted him with good lungs, large eyes, and a hook nose; his success before barn audiences was consequently brilliant. His professional exertions, it must be owned, barely sufficed to feed and clothe him; but then he had a triumph on the London stage, always present in the far perspective to console him. While waiting this desirable event, he indulged himself in a little intermediate luxury, much in favour as a profitable resource for young men in extreme difficulties – he married; married at the age of nineteen, or thereabouts, the charming Columbine of the company.

And he got a good wife. Many people, I know, will refuse to believe this, – it is a truth, nevertheless. The one redeeming success of the vast social failure which his whole existence was doomed to represent, was this very marriage of his with a strolling Columbine. She, poor girl, toiled as hard and as cheerfully to get her own bread after marriage, as before; trudged many a weary mile by his side from town to town, and never uttered a complaint; praised his acting; partook his hopes; patched his clothes; pardoned his ill-humour; paid court for him to his manager; made up his squabbles; – in a word, and in the best and highest sense of that word, loved him. May I be allowed to add, that she only brought him one child – a girl? And, considering the state of his pecuniary resources, am I justified in ranking this circumstance as a strong additional proof of her excellent qualities as a married woman?

After much perseverance and many disappointments, Reuben at last succeeded in attaching himself to a regular provincial company – Tate Wilkinson's at York. He had to descend low enough from his original dramatic pedestal, before he succeeded in subduing the manager. From the leading business in Tragedy and Melodrama, he sank at once, in the established provincial company, to a 'minor utility,' – words of theatrical slang signifying an actor who is put to the smaller dramatic uses which the necessities of the stage require. Still, in spite of this, he persisted in hoping for the chance that was never to come; and still poor Columbine faithfully hoped with him to the last.

Time passed – years of it; and this chance never arrived; and he and Columbine found themselves one day in London, forlorn and starving. Their life at this period would make a romance of itself, if I had time and space to write it; but I must get on, as fast as may be, to later dates; and the reader must be contented merely to know that, at the last gasp – the last of hope; almost the last of life – Reuben got employment, as an actor of the lower degree, at Drury Lane.

Behold him, then, now – still a young man, but crushed in his young man's ambition for ever – receiving the lowest theatrical wages for the lowest theatrical work; appearing on the stage as soldier, waiter, footman, and so on; with not a line in the play to speak; just showing his poverty-shrunken carcase to the audience, clothed in the frowsiest habiliments of the old Drury Lane wardrobe, for a minute or two at a time, at something like a shilling a night – a miserable being, in a miserable world; the World behind the Scenes!

John Philip Kemble is now acting at the theatre: and his fame is rising to its climax. How the roar of applause follows him almost every time he leaves the scene! How majestically he stalks away into the Green Room, abstractedly inhaling his huge pinches of snuff as he goes! How the poor inferior brethren of the buskin, as they stand at the wing and stare upon him reverently, long for his notice; and how few of them can possibly get it! There is, nevertheless, one among this tribe of unfortunates whom he has really remarked, though he has not yet spoken to him. He has detected this man, shabby and solitary, constantly studying his acting from any vantage-ground the poor wretch could get amid the dust, dirt, draughts, and confusion behind the scenes. Mr Kemble also observes, that whenever a play of Shakspeare's is being acted, this stranger has a tattered old book in his hands; and appears to be following the performance closely from the text, instead of huddling into warm corners over a pint of small beer, with the rest of his supernumerary brethren. Remarking these things, Mr Kemble over and over again intends to speak to the man, and find out who he is; and over and over again utterly forgets it. But, at last, a day comes when the long-deferred personal communication really takes place; and it happens thus:–

A new Tragedy is to be produced – a pre-eminently bad one, by-the-by, even in those days of pre-eminently bad Tragedy-writing. The scene is laid in Scotland; and Mr Kemble is determined to play his part in a Highland dress. The idea of acting a drama in the appropriate costume of the period which that drama illustrates, is considered so dangerous an innovation, that no one else dare follow his example; and he, of all the characters, is actually about to wear the only Highland dress in a Highland play.* This does not at all daunt him. He has acted Othello, a night or two before, in the uniform of a British General Officer,† and is so conscious of the enormous absurdity of the thing, that he is determined to persevere, and start the reform in stage costume, which he was afterwards determined so thoroughly to carry out.

* A fact! See Boaden's *Life of Kemble*, vol. i. p. 326.
† Another fact!! See the same work, vol. i. p. 256.

The night comes; the play begins. Just as the stage waits for Mr Kemble, Mr Kemble discovers that his goat-skin purse – one of the most striking peculiarities of the Highland dress – is not on him. There is no time to seek it – all is lost for the cause of costume! – he must go on the stage exposed to public view as only half a Highlander! No! Not yet! While everybody else hurries frantically hither and thither in vain, one man quickly straps something about Mr Kemble's waist, just in the nick of time. It is the lost purse! and Roscius after all steps on the stage, a Highlander complete from top to toe!

On his first exit, Mr Kemble inquires for the man who found the purse. It is that very poor player whom he has already remarked. The great actor had actually been carrying the purse about in his own hands before the performance; and, in a moment of abstraction, had put it down on a chair, in a dark place behind the prompter's box. The humble admirer, noticing everything he did, noticed this; and so found the missing goatskin in time, when nobody else could.

'Sir, I am infinitely obliged to you,' says Mr Kemble, courteously, to the confused, blushing man before him — 'You have saved me from appearing incomplete, and therefore ridiculous, before a Drury Lane audience. I have marked you, sir, before; reading, while waiting for your call, our divine Shakspeare – the poetic bond that unites all men, however professional distance may separate them. Accept, sir, this offered pinch – this pinch of snuff.'

When the penniless player went home that night, what wonderful news he had for his wife! And how proud and happy poor Columbine was, when she heard that Reuben Wray had been offered a pinch of snuff out of Mr Kemble's own box!

But the kind-hearted tragedian did not stop merely at a fine speech and a social condescension. Reuben read Shakspeare, when none of his comrades would have cared to look into the book at all; and that of itself was enough to make him interesting to Mr Kemble. Besides, he was a young man; and might have capacities which only wanted encouragement.

'I beg you to recite to me, sir,' said the great John Philip, one night; desirous of seeing what his humble admirer really could do. The result of the recitation was unequivocal: poor Wray could do nothing that hundreds of his brethren could not have equalled. In him, the yearning to become a great actor was only the ambition without the power.

Still, Reuben gained something by the goat-skin purse. A timely word from his new protector raised him two or three degrees higher in the Company, and increased his salary in proportion. He got parts now with some lines to speak in them; and – condescension on condescension! – Mr Kemble actually declaimed them for his instruction at rehearsal, and solemnly showed him (oftener, I am afraid, in jest than earnest) how a patriotic Roman soldier, or a bereaved father's faithful footman, should tread the stage.

These instructions were always received by the grateful Wray in the most perfect good faith; and it was precisely in virtue of his lessons thus derived – numbering about half-a-dozen, and lasting about two minutes each – that he afterwards advertised himself, as teacher of elocution and pupil of John Kemble. Many a great man has blazed away famously before the public eye, as pupil of some other great man, from no larger a supply of original educational fuel than belonged to Mr Reuben Wray.

Having fairly traced our friend to his connexion with Mr Kemble, I may dismiss the rest of his advertisement more briefly. All, I suppose, that you now want further explained, is:– How he came to teach elocution, and how he got on by teaching it.

Well: Reuben stuck fast to Drury Lane Theatre through rivalries, and quarrels, and disasters, and fluctuations in public taste, which overthrew more important interests than his own. The theatre was rebuilt, and burnt, and rebuilt again; and still Old Wray (as he now began to be called) was part and parcel of the establishment, however others might desert it. During this long lapse of monotonous years, affliction and death preyed cruelly on the poor actor's home. First, his kind, patient Columbine died; then, after a long interval, Columbine's only child married early; – and woe is me! – married a sad rascal, who first ill-treated and then deserted her. She soon followed her mother to the grave, leaving one girl – the little Annie of this story – to Reuben's care. One of the first things her grandfather taught the child was to call herself Annie *Wray*. He never could endure hearing her dissolute father's name pronounced by any body; and was resolved that she should always bear his own.

Ah! what woeful times were those for the poor player! How many a night he sat in the darkest corner behind the scenes, with his tattered Shakspeare – the only thing about him he had never pawned – in his hand, and the tears rolling down his hollow, painted cheeks, as he thought on the dear lost Columbine, and Columbine's child! How often those tears still stood thick in his eyes when he marched across the stage at the head of a mock army, or hobbled up to deliver the one eternal letter to the one eternal dandy hero of high Comedy! – Comedy, indeed! If the people before the lamps, who were roaring with laughter at the fun of the mercurial fine gentleman of the play, had only seen what was tugging at the heart of the miserable old stage footman who brought him his chocolate and newspapers, all the wit in the world would not have saved the comedy from being wept over as the most affecting tragedy that was ever written.

But the time was to come – long after this, however – when Reuben's connexion with the theatre was to cease. As if fate had ironically bound up together the stage-destinies of the great actor and the small, the year of Mr Kemble's retirement from the boards, was the year of Mr Wray's dismissal from them.

He had been, for some time past, getting too old to be useful – then, the theatrical world in which he had been bred was altering, and he could not alter with it. A little man with fiery black eyes, whose name was Edmund Kean, had come up from the country and blazed like a comet through the thick old conventional mists of the English stage. From that time, the new school began to rise, and the old school to sink; and Reuben went down, with other insignificant atoms, in the vortex. At the end of the season, he was informed that his services were no longer required.

It was then, when he found himself once more forlorn in the world – almost as forlorn as when he had first come to London with poor Columbine – that the notion of trying elocution struck him. He had a little sum of money to begin with, subscribed for him by his richer brethren when he left the theatre. Why might he not get on as a teacher of elocution in the country, just as some of his superior fellow-players got on in the same vocation in London? Necessity whispered, Doubt not, but try. He had a grandchild to support – so he did try.

His method of teaching was exceedingly simple. He had one remedy for the deficiencies of every class whom he addressed – the Kemble remedy: he had watched Mr Kemble year by year, till he knew every inch of him; and, so to speak, had learnt him by heart. Did a pupil want to walk the stage properly? – teach him Mr Kemble's walk. Did a rising politician want to become impressive as an orator? – teach him Mr Kemble's gesticulations in Brutus. So again, with regard to strictly vocal necessities. Did gentleman number one, wish to learn the art of reading aloud? – let him learn the Kemble cadences. Did gentleman number two, feel weak in his pronunciation? – let him sound vowels, consonants, and crack-jaw syllables, just as Mr Kemble sounded them on the stage. And, out of what book were they to be taught? – from what manual were the clergymen and orators, the aspirants for dramatic fame, the young ladies whose delivery was ungraceful, the young gentlemen whose diction was improper, to be all alike improved! From Shakspeare – every one of them from Shakspeare! He had no idea of anything else: literature meant Shakspeare to *him*. It was his great glory and triumph, that he had Shakspeare by heart. All that he knew, every tender and loveable recollection, every small honour he had gained in his own poor blank sphere, was somehow sure to be associated with William Shakspeare!

And why not? What is Shakspeare but a great sun that shines upon humanity – the large heads and the little, alike? Have not the rays of that

m... ...nto many poor and lowly places for good? What
...fall, pleasant and invigorating, even upon

...with Shakspeare for his textbook, and Mr
...our friend in his old age bravely invaded
...teacher of elocution, with all its supplementary
...nd, wonderful to relate, though occasionally
...ivations, he just managed to make elocution – or
...d of it with his patrons – keep his grandchild and

...that any orators or clergymen anxiously demanded secret
improvement from him (see advertisement) at three-and-sixpence an
hour; or that young ladies sought the graces of delivery, and young
gentlemen the proprieties of diction (see advertisement again) from his
experienced tongue. But he got on in other ways, nevertheless.
Sometimes he was hired to drill the boys on a speech-day at a country
school. Sometimes he was engaged to prevent provincial amateur actors
from murdering the dialogue outright, and incessantly jostling each other
on the stage. In this last capacity, he occasionally got good employment,
especially with regular amateur societies, who found his terms cheap
enough, and his knowledge of theatrical discipline inestimably useful.

But chances like these were as nothing to the chances he got when he
was occasionally employed to superintend all the toilsome part of the
business in arranging private theatricals at country houses. Here, he met
with greater generosity than he had ever dared to expect: here, the letter
from Mr Kemble, vouching for his honesty and general stage-knowledge –
the great actor's last legacy of kindness to him, which he carried about
everywhere – was sure to produce prodigious effect. He and little Annie,
and a third member of the family whom I shall hereafter introduce, lived
for months together on the proceeds of such a windfall as a private
theatrical party – for the young people, in the midst of their amusement,
found leisure to pity the poor old ex-player, and to admire his pretty
grand-daughter; and liberally paid him for his services full five times as
much as he would ever have ventured to ask.

Thus, wandering about from town to town, sometimes miserably
unsuccessful, sometimes re-animated by a little prosperity, he had come
from Stratford-upon-Avon, while the present century was some twenty-
five years younger than it is now, to try his luck at elocution with the
people of Tidbury-on-the-Marsh – to teach the graces of delivery at
seventy years of age, with half his teeth gone! Will he succeed? I, for one,
hope so. There is something in the spectacle of this poor old man, sorely
battered by the world, yet still struggling for life, and for the grandchild
he loves better than life – struggling hard, himself a remnant of a bygone

age, to keep up with a new age which has already got past him, and will hardly hear his feeble voice of other times, except to laugh at it – there is surely something in this which forbids all thought of ridicule, and bids fair with every body for compassion and good-will.

But we have had talk enough, by this time, about Mr Reuben Wray. Let us now go at once and make acquaintance with him – not forgetting his mysterious cash-box – at No. 12.

CHAPTER III

MR WRAY AND HIS FAMILY

The breakfast-things are laid in the little drawing-room at Reuben's lodgings. This drawing-room, observe, has not been hired by our friend; he never possessed such a domestic luxury in his life. The apartment, not being taken, has only been lent to him by his landlady, who is hugely impressed by the tragic suavity of her new tenant's manner and 'delivery.' The breakfast-things, I say again, are laid. Three cups, a loaf, half-a-pound of salt butter, some moist sugar in a saucer, and a black earthenware tea-pot, with a broken spout; such are the sumptuous preparations which tempt Mr Wray and his family to come down at nine o'clock in the morning, and yet nobody appears!

Hark! there is a sound of creaking boots, descending, apparently, from some loft at the top of the house, so distant is the noise they make at first. This sound, coming heavily nearer and nearer, only stops at the drawing-room door, and heralds the entry of——

Mr Wray, of course? No! – no such luck: my belief is, that we shall never succeed in getting to Mr Wray personally. The individual in question is not even any relation of his; but he is a member of the family for all that; and as the first to come down stairs, he certainly merits the reward of immediate notice.

He is nearly six feet high, proportionately strong and stout, and looks about thirty years of age. His gait is as awkward as it well can be; his features are large and ill-proportioned, his face is pitted with the small-pox, and what hair he has on his head – not much – seems to be growing in all sorts of contrary directions at once. I know nothing about him, personally, that I can praise, but his expression; and that is so thoroughly good-humoured, so candid, so innocent even, that it really makes amends for everything else. Honesty and kindliness look out so brightly from his eyes, as to dazzle your observation of his clumsy nose, and lumpy mouth and chin, until you hardly know whether they are ugly or not. Some men, in a certain sense, are ugly with the lineaments of the Apollo Belvidere; and others handsome, with features that might sit for a caricature. Our new acquaintance was of the latter order.

Allow me to introduce him to you: – THE GENTLE READER – JULIUS CAESAR. Stop! start not at those classic syllables; I will explain all.

The history of Mr Martin Blunt, *alias* 'Julius Caesar,' is a good deal like the history of Mr Reuben Wray. Like him, Blunt began life with strolling players – not, however, as an actor, but as stage-carpenter, candle-snuffer, door-keeper, and general errand-boy. On one occasion, when the company were ambitiously bent on the horrible profanation of performing Shakspeare's Julius Caesar, the actor who was to personate the emperor fell ill. Nobody was left to suppy his place – every other available member of the company was engaged in the play; so, in despair, they resorted to Martin Blunt. He was big enough for a Roman hero; and that was all they looked to.

They first cut out as much of his part as they could, and then half crammed the rest into his reluctant brains; they clapped a white sheet about the poor lad's body for a toga, stuck a truncheon into his hand, and a short beard on his chin; and remorselessly pushed him on the stage. His performance was received with shouts of laughter; but he went through it; was duly assassinated; and fell with a thump that shook the surrounding scenery to its centre, and got him a complete round of applause all to himself.

He never forgot this. It was his first and last appearance; and, in the innocence of his heart, he boasted of it on every occasion, as the great distinction of his life. When he found his way to London; and as a really skilful carpenter, procured employment at Drury Lane, his fellow-workmen managed to get the story of his first performance out of him directly, and made a standing joke of it. He was elected a general butt, and nick-named 'Julius Caesar,' by universal acclamation. Everybody conferred on him that classic title; and I only follow the general fashion in these pages. If you don't like the name, call him any other you please: he is too good-humoured to be offended with you, do what you will.

He was thus introduced to old Wray:–

At the time when Reuben was closing his career at Drury Lane, our stout young carpenter had just begun work there. One night, about a week before the performance of a new Pantomime, some of the heavy machinery tottered just as Wray was passing by it; and would have fallen on him, but for 'Julius Caesar,' (I really can't call him Blunt!), who, at the risk of his own limbs, caught the tumbling mass; and by a tremendous exertion of main strength arrested it in its fall, till the old man had hobbled out of harm's way. This led to gratitude, friendship, intimacy.

Wray and his preserver, in spite of the difference in their characters and ages, seemed to suit each other, somehow. In fine, when Reuben started to teach elocution in the country, the carpenter followed him, as protector, assistant, servant, or whatever you please.

'Julius Caesar' had one special motive for attaching himself to old Wray's fortunes, which will speedily appear, when little Annie enters the drawing-room. Awkward as he might be, he was certainly no encumbrance. He made himself useful and profitable in fifty different ways. He took round hand-bills soliciting patronage; constructed the scenery when Mr Wray got private theatrical engagements; worked as journeyman-carpenter when other resources failed; and was, in fact, ready for anything, from dunning for a bad debt, to cleaning a pair of boots. His master might at times be as fretful as he pleased, and treat him like an infant during occasional fits of crossness – he never replied, and never looked sulky. The only things he could not be got to do, were to abstain from inadvertently knocking everything down that came in his reach, and to improve the action of his arms and legs on the principle of the late Mr Kemble.

Let us return to the drawing-room, and the breakfast-things. 'Julius Caesar,' of the creaking boots, came into the room with a small work-box (which he had been secretly engaged in making for some time past) in one hand, and a new muslin cravat in the other. It was Annie's birthday. The box was a present; the cravat, what the French would call, a homage to the occasion.

His first proceeding was to drop the work-box, and pick it up again in a great hurry; his second, to go to the looking glass (no such piece of furniture ornamented his loft bedroom,) and try to put on the new cravat. He had only half tied it, and was hesitating, utterly helpless, over the bow, when a light step sounded on the floor-cloth outside. Annie came in.

'Julius Caesar at the looking-glass! Oh, good gracious, what *can* have come to him!' exclaimed the little girl with a merry laugh.

How fresh, and blooming, and pretty she looked, as she ran up the next moment; and telling him to stoop, tied his cravat directly – standing on tiptoe. 'There,' she cried, 'now that's done, what have you got to say to me, sir, on my birth-day!'

'I've got a box; and I'm so glad it's your birthday,' says 'Julius Caesar', too confused by the suddenness of the cravat-tying to know exactly what he is talking about.

'Oh, what a splendid work-box! how kind of you, to be sure! what care I shall take of it! Come, sir, I suppose I must tell you to give me a kiss after that,' and, standing on tiptoe again, she held up her fresh, rosy cheek to be kissed, with such a pretty mixture of bashfulness, gratitude, and arch enjoyment in her look, that 'Julius Caesar,' I regret to say, felt inclined then and there to go down upon both his knees and worship her outright.

Before the decorous reader has time to consider all this very improper, I had better, perhaps, interpose a word, and explain that Annie Wray had promised Martin Blunt, (I give his real name again here, because this is serious business,) yes; had actually promised him that one day she would be his wife. She kept all her promises; but I can tell you she was especially determined to keep this.

Impossible! exclaims the lady reader. With her good looks she might aspire many degrees above a poor carpenter; besides, how could she possibly care about a great lumpish, awkward fellow, who *is* ugly, say what you will about his expression?

I might reply, madam, that our little Annie had looked rather deeper than the skin in choosing her husband; and had found out certain qualities of heart and disposition about this poor carpenter, which made her love, – aye, and respect and admire him too. But I prefer asking you a question, by way of answer. Did you never meet with any individuals of your own sex, lovely, romantic, magnificent young women, who have fairly stupified the whole circle of their relatives and friends by marrying particularly short, scrubby, matter-of-fact, middle-aged men, showing, too, every symptom of fondness for them into the bargain? I fancy you must have seen such cases as I have mentioned; and, when you can explain them to *my* satisfaction, I shall be happy to explain the anomalous engagement of little Annie to *yours*.

In the meantime it may be well to relate, that this odd love affair was only once hinted at to Mr Wray. The old man flew into a frantic passion directly; and threatened dire extremities if the thing was ever thought of more. Lonely, and bereaved of all other ties, as he was, he had, in regard to his grand-daughter, that jealousy of other people loving her, which is of all weaknesses, in such cases as his, the most pardonable and the most pure. If a duke had asked for Annie in marriage, I doubt very much whether Mr Wray would have let him have her, except upon the understanding that they were all to live together.

Under these circumstances, the engagement was never hinted at again. Annie told her lover they must wait, and be patient, and remain as brother and sister to one another, till better chances and better times came. And 'Julius Caesar' listened, and strictly obeyed. He was a good deal like a large, faithful dog to his little betrothed: he loved her, watched over her, guarded her, with his whole heart and strength; only asking in return, the privilege of fulfilling her slightest wish.

Well; this kiss, about which I have been digressing so long, was fortunately just over, when another footstep sounded outside; the door

opened; and – yes! we have got him at last, in his own proper person!
Enter Mr Reuben Wray!

Age has given him a stoop, which he tries to conceal, but cannot. His
cheeks are hollow; his face is seamed with wrinkles, the work not only of
time, but of trial, too. Still, there is vitality of mind, courage of heart
about the old man, even yet. His look has not lost all its animation, nor
his smile its worth. *There* is the true Kemble walk, and the true Kemble
carriage of the head for you, if you like! – *there* is the second-hand tragic
grandeur and propriety, which the unfortunate 'Julius Caesar' daily
contemplates, yet cannot even faintly copy! Look at his dress, again.
Threadbare as it is (patched, I am afraid, in some places), there is not a
speck of dust on it, and what little hair is left on his bald head is carefully
brushed as if he rejoiced in the love-locks of Absalom himself. No!
though misfortune, and disappointment, and grief, and heavy-handed
penury have all been assailing him ruthlessly enough for more than half a
century, they have not got the brave old fellow down yet! At seventy
years of age he is still on his legs in the Prize-Ring of Life; badly
punished all over (as the pugilists say), but determined to win the fight to
the last!

'Many happy returns of the day, my love,' says old Reuben, going up to
Annie, and kissing her. 'This is the twentieth birthday of yours I've lived
to see. Thank God for that!'

'Look at my present, grandfather,' cries the little girl, proudly showing
her work-box. 'Can you guess who made it?'

'You are a good fellow, Julius Caesar!' exclaims Mr Wray, guessing
directly. 'Good morning; shake hands.' – (Then, in a lower voice to
Annie) – 'Has he broken anything in particular, since he's been up?' 'No!'
'I'm very glad to hear it. Julius Caesar, let me offer you a pinch of snuff,'
and here he pulled out his box quite in the Kemble style. He had his
natural manner, and his Kemble manner. The first only appeared when
anything greatly pleased or affected him – the second was for those
ordinary occasions when he had time to remember that he was a teacher
of elocution, and a pupil of the English Roscius.

'Thank ye, kindly, sir,' said the gratified carpenter, cautiously advancing
his huge finger and thumb towards the offered box.

'Stop!' cried old Wray, suddenly withdrawing it. He always lectured to
'Julius Caesar' on elocution when he had nobody else to teach, just to
keep his hand in. 'Stop! that won't do. In the first place, "Thank ye,
kindly, sir." though good-humoured, is grossly inelegant. "Sir, I am
obliged to you," is the proper phrase – mind you sound the *i* in obliged –
never say *obleeged*, as some people do; and remember, what I am now
telling *you*, Mr Kemble once said to the Prince Regent! The next hint I
have to give is this – never take your pinch of snuff with your right hand

finger and thumb; it should be always the left. Perhaps you would like to know why?'

'Yes, please, sir,' says the admiring disciple, very humbly.

'"Yes, *if* you please, sir," would have been better; but let that pass as a small error. – And now, I will tell you why, in an anecdote. Matthews was one day mimicking Mr Kemble to his face, in Penruddock – the great scene where he stops to take a pinch of snuff. "Very good, Matthews; very like me," says Mr Kemble complacently, when Matthews had done; "but you have made one great mistake." "What's that?" cries Matthews sharply. "My friend, you have not represented me taking snuff like a gentleman: now, I always do. You took your pinch, in imitating my Penruddock, with your right hand: I use my *left* – a gentleman invariably does, because then he has his right hand always clean from tobacco to give to his friend!" – There! remember that: and now you may take your pinch.'

Mr Wray next turned round to speak to Annie; but his voice was instantly drowned in a perfect explosion of sneezes, absolutely screamed out by the unhappy 'Julius Caesar,' whose nasal nerves were convulsed by the snuff. Mentally determining never to offer his box to his faithful follower again, old Reuben gave up making his proposed remark, until they were all quietly seated round the breakfast-table: then, he returned to the charge with renewed determination.

'Annie, my dear,' said he, 'you and I have read a great deal together of our divine Shakspeare, as Mr Kemble always called him. You are my regular pupil, you know, and ought to be able to quote by this time almost as much as I can. I am going to try you with something quite new – suppose I had offered *you* the pinch of snuff (Mr Julius Caesar shall never have another, I can promise him); what would you have said from Shakspeare applicable to *that?* Just think now!'

'But, grandfather, snuff wasn't invented in Shakspeare's time – was it?' said Annie.

'That's of no consequence,' retorted the old man: 'Shakspeare was for *all* time: you can quote him for everything in the world, as long as the world lasts. Can't you quote him for snuff? I can. Now, listen. You say to me, "I offer you a pinch of snuff?" I answer from Cymbeline (Act iv. scene 2): – "Pisanio! I'll now taste of thy drug." There! won't that do? What's snuff but a drug for the nose? It just fits – everything of the divine Shakspeare's does, when you know him by heart, as I do – eh, little Annie? And now give me some more sugar; I wish it was lump for *your* sake, dear; but I'm afraid we can only afford moist. Anybody called about the advertisement? a new pupil this morning – eh?'

No! no pupils at all: not a man, woman, or child in the town, to teach elocution to yet! Mr Wray was not at all despondent about this; he had made up his mind that a pupil must come in the course of the day; and that was enough for him. His little quibbling from Shakspeare about the snuff had put him in the best of good humours. He went on making quotations, talking elocution, and eating bread and butter, as brisk and happy, as if all Tidbury had combined to form one mighty class for him, and resolved to pay ready money for every lesson.

But after breakfast, when the things were taken away, the old man seemed suddenly to recollect something which changed his manner altogether. He grew first embarrassed; then silent; then pulled out his Shakspeare, and began to read with ostentatious assiduity, as if he were especially desirous that nobody should speak to him.

At the same time, a close observer might have detected Mr 'Julius Caesar' making various uncouth signs and grimaces to Annie, which the little girl apparently understood, but did not know how to answer. At last, with an effort, as if she were summoning extraordinary resolution, she said:– 'Grandfather – you have not forgotten your promise?'

No answer from Mr Wray. Probably, he was too much absorbed over Shakspeare to hear.

'Grandfather,' repeated Annie, in a louder tone; 'you promised to explain a certain mystery to us, on my birthday.'

Mr Wray was obliged to hear this time. He looked up with a very perplexed face.

'Yes, dear,' said he, 'I did promise; but I almost wish I had not. It's rather a dangerous mystery to explain, little Annie, I can tell you! Why should you be so very curious to know about it?'

'I'm sure, grandfather,' pleaded Annie, 'you can't say I am over-curious, or Julius Caesar either, in wanting to know it. Just recollect – we had been only three days at Stratford-upon-Avon, when you came in, looking so dreadfully frightened, and said we must go away directly. And you made us pack up; and we all went off in a hurry, more like prisoners escaping, than honest people.'

'We did!' groaned old Reuben, beginning to look like a culprit already.

'Well,' continued Annie; 'and you wouldn't tell us a word of what it was all for, beg as hard as we might. And then, when we asked why you never let that old cash-box (which I used to keep my odds and ends in) out of your own hands, after we left Stratford – you wouldn't tell us that, either, and ordered us never to mention the thing again. It was only in one of your particular good humours, that I just got you to promise you would tell us all about it on my next birthday – to celebrate the day, you said. I'm sure we are to be trusted with any secrets; and I don't think it's being very curious to want to know this.'

'Very well!' said Mr Wray, rising, with a sort of desperate calmness; 'I've promised, and, come what may, I'll keep my promise. Wait here; I'll be back directly.' And he left the room, in a great hurry.

He returned immediately, with the cash-box. A very battered, shabby affair, to make such a mystery about! thought Annie, as he put the box on the table, and solemnly laid his hands across it.

'Now, then,' said old Wray, in his deepest tragedy-tones, and with very serious looks; 'Promise me, on your word of honour – both of you – that you'll never say a word of what I'm going to tell, to anybody, on any account whatever – I don't care what happens – *on any account whatever!*'

Annie and her lover gave their promises directly, and very seriously. They were getting a little agitated by all these elaborate preparations for the coming disclosure.

'Shut the door!' said Mr Wray, in a stage whisper. 'Now sit close and listen; I'm ready to explain the mystery.'

CHAPTER IV

THE MYSTERY OF THE CASH-BOX

'I suppose,' said old Reuben, 'you have neither of you forgotten that, on the second day of our visit to Stratford, I went out in the afternoon to dine with an intimate friend of mine, whom I'd known from a boy, and who lived at some little distance from the town——'

'Forget that!' cried Annie! – 'I don't think we ever shall – I was frightened about you, all the time you were gone.'

'Frightened about what?' asked Mr Wray sharply. 'Do you mean to tell me, Annie, you suspected——'

'I don't know what I suspected, grandfather; but I thought your going away by yourself, to sleep at your friend's house (as you told us), and not to come back till the next morning, something very extraordinary. It was the first time we had ever slept under different roofs – only think of that!'

'I'm ashamed to say, my dear' – rejoined Mr Wray, suddenly beginning to look and speak very uneasily – 'that I turned hypocrite, and something worse, too, on that occasion. I deceived you. I had no friend to go and dine with; and I didn't pass the night in any house at all.'

'Grandfather!' cried Annie, jumping up in a fright – 'What *can* you mean!'

'Beg pardon, sir,' added 'Julius Caesar,' turning very red, and slowly clenching both his enormous fists as he spoke – 'Beg pardon; but if you was put upon, or made fun of by any chaps that night, I wish you'd just please to tell me where I could find 'em.'

'Nobody ill-used me,' said the old man, in steady, and even solemn tones. 'I passed the night by the grave of William Shakspeare, in Stratford-upon-Avon Church!'

Annie sank back into her seat, and lost all her pretty complexion in a moment. The worthy carpenter gave such a start, that he broke the back rail of his chair. – It was a variation on his usual performances of this sort, which were generally confined to cups, saucers, and wine-glasses.

Mr Wray took no notice of the accident. This was of itself enough to show that he was strongly agitated by something. After a momentary silence, he spoke again, completely forgetting the Kemble manner and the Kemble elocution, as he went on.

'I say again, I passed all that night in Stratford Church; and you shall know for what. You went with me, Annie, in the morning – it was Tuesday: yes, Tuesday morning – to see Shakspeare's bust in the church. *You* looked at it, like other people, just as a curiosity – *I* looked at it, as the greatest treasure in the world; the only true likeness of Shakspeare! It's been done from a mask, taken from his own face, after death – I know it: I don't care what people say, I know it. Well, when we went home, I felt as if I'd seen Shakspeare himself, risen from the dead! Strangers would laugh if I told them so; but it's true – I *did* feel it. And this thought came across me, quick, like the shooting of a sudden pain: – I must make that face of Shakspeare mine; my possession, my companion, my great treasure that no money can pay for! And I've got it! – Here! – the only cast in the world from the Stratford bust is locked up in this old cash-box!'

He paused a moment. Astonishment kept both his auditors silent.

'You both know,' he continued, 'that I was bred apprentice to a statuary. Among other things, he taught me to take casts: it was part of our business – the easiest part. I knew I could take a mould off the Stratford bust, if I had the courage; and the courage came to me: on the Tuesday, it came. I went and bought some plaster, some soft soap, and a quart basin – those were my materials – and tied them up together in an old canvas bag. Water was all I wanted besides; and that I saw in the church vestry, in the morning – a jug of it, left I suppose since Sunday, where it had been put for the clergyman's use. I could carry my bag under my cloak quite comfortably, you understand. The only thing that troubled me now was how to get into the church again, without being suspected. While I was thinking, I passed the inn door. Some people were on the steps, talking to some other people in the street: they were making an appointment to go all together, and see Shakspeare's bust and grave that very afternoon. This was enough for me: I determined to go into the church with them.'

'What! and stop there all night, grandfather?'

'And stop there all night, Annie. Taking a mould, you know, is not a very long business; but I wanted to take mine unobserved; and the early morning, before anybody was up, was the only time to do that safely in the church. Besides, I wanted plenty of leisure, because I wasn't sure I should succeed at first, after being out of practice so long in making casts. But you shall hear how I did it, when the time comes. Well, I made up the story about dining and sleeping at my friend's, because I didn't know what might happen, and because – because, in short, I didn't like to tell you what I was going to do. So I went out secretly, near the church; and waited for the party coming. They were late – late in the afternoon, before they came. We all went in together; I with my bag, you know, hid under my cloak. The man who showed us over the church in the morning, luckily for me, wasn't there: an old woman took his duty for him in the afternoon. I waited till the visitors were all congregated round Shakspeare's grave, bothering the poor woman with foolish questions about him. I knew that was my time, and slipped off into the vestry, and opened the cupboard, and hid myself among the surplices, as quiet as a mouse. After awhile, I heard one of the strangers in the church (they were very rude, boisterous people) asking the other, what had become of the "old fogey with the cloak?" and the other answered that he must have gone out, like a wise man, and that they had all better go after him, for it was precious cold and dull in the church. They went away: I heard the doors shut, and knew I was locked in for the night.'

'All night in a church! Oh, grandfather, how frightened you must have been!'

'Well, Annie, I was a little frightened; but more at what I was going to do, than at being alone in the church. Let me get on with my story though. Being autumn weather, it grew too dark after the people went, for me to do anything then; so I screwed my courage up to wait for the morning. The first thing I did was to go and look quietly, all by myself, at the bust; and I made up my mind that I could take the mould in about three or four pieces. All I wanted was what they call a *mask*: that means just a forehead and face, without the head. It's an easy thing to take a mask off a bust – I knew I could do it; but, somehow, I didn't feel quite comfortable just then. The bust began to look very awful to me, in the fading light, all alone in the church. It was almost like looking at the ghost of Shakspeare, in that place, and at that time. If the door hadn't been locked, I think I should have run out of the church; but I couldn't do that; so I knelt down and kissed the grave-stone – a curious fancy coming over me as I did so, that it was like wishing Shakspeare good night – and then I groped my way back to the vestry. When I got in, and had shut the door between me and the grave, I grew bolder, I can tell you; and thought to myself – I'm doing no harm; I'm not going to hurt the bust; I only want what an Englishman and an old actor may fairly covet, a copy of Shakspeare's face; why shouldn't I eat my bit of supper here, and say my prayers as usual, and get my nap into the bargain, if I can? Just as I thought that – BANG went the clock, striking the hour! It almost knocked me down, bold as I felt the moment before. I was obliged to wait till it was all still again, before I could pull the bit of bread and cheese I had got with me out of my pocket. And when I did, I couldn't eat: I was too impatient for the morning; so I sat down in the parson's arm-chair; and tried, next, whether I could sleep at all.'

'And could you, grandfather?'

'No – I couldn't sleep either; at least, not at first. It was quite dark now; and I began to feel cold and awe-struck again. The only thing I could think of to keep up my spirits at all, was first saying my prayers, and then quoting Shakspeare. I went at it, Annie, like a dragon; play after play – except the tragedies; I was afraid of *them*, in a church at night, all by myself. Well: I think I had got half through the Midsummer Night's Dream, whispering over bit after bit of it; when I whispered myself into a doze. Then I fell into a queer sleep; and then I had such a dream! I dreamt that the church was full of moonlight – brighter moonlight than ever I saw awake. I walked out of the vestry; and there were the fairies of the Midsummer Night's Dream – all creatures like sparks of silver light – dancing round the Shakspeare bust! The moment they caught sight of me, they all called out in their sweet nightingale voices: – 'Come along, Reuben! sly old Reuben! we know what you're here for, and we don't mind you a bit! You love Shakspeare, and so do we – dance, Reuben, and be happy! Shakspeare likes an old actor; he was an actor himself – nobody sees us! we're out for the night! foot it, old Reuben – foot it away!' And we all danced like mad: now, up in the air; now, down on the pavement; and now, all round the bust five hundred thousand times at least without stopping, till – BANG went the clock! and I woke up in the dark, in a cold perspiration.'

'I'm in one too!' gasped 'Julius Caesar,' dabbing his brow vehemently with a ragged cotton pocket-handkerchief.

'Well, after that dream I fell to reciting again; and got another doze; and had another dream – a terrible one, about ghosts and witches, that I don't recollect so well as the other. I woke up once more, cold, and in a great fright that I'd slept away all the precious morning daylight. No! all dark still! I went into the church again, and then back to the vestry, not being able to stay there. I suppose I did this a dozen times without knowing why. At last, never going to sleep again, I got somehow through the night – the night that seemed never to be done. Soon after daybreak, I began to walk up and down the church briskly, to get myself warm, keeping at it for a long time. Then, just as I saw through the windows that the sun was rising, I opened my bag at last, and got ready for work. I can tell you my hand trembled and my sight grew dim – I think the tears were in my eyes; but I don't know why – as I first soaped the bust all over to prevent the plaster I was going to put on it from sticking. Then I mixed up the plaster and water in my quart basin, taking care to leave no lumps, and finding it come as natural to me as if I had only left the statuary's shop yesterday; then – but it's no use telling you, little Annie, about what you don't understand; I'd better say shortly I made the mould, in four pieces, as I thought I should – two for the upper part of the face, and two for the lower. Then, having put on the outer plaster case to hold the mould, I pulled all off clean together, and looked, and knew that I had got a mask of Shakspeare from the Stratford bust!'

'Oh, grandfather, how glad you must have been then!'

'No, that was the odd part of it. At first, I felt as if I had robbed the bank, or the King's jewels, or had set fire to a train of gunpowder to blow up all London; it seemed such a thing to have done! Such a tremendously daring, desperate thing! But, a little while after, a frantic sort of joy came over me: I could hardly prevent myself from shouting and singing at the top of my voice. Then I felt a perfect fever of impatience to cast the mould directly; and see whether the mask would come out without a flaw. The keeping down that impatience was the hardest thing I had had to do since I first got into the church.'

'But, please, sir, whenever did you get out at last? Do pray tell us that!' asked 'Julius Caesar.'

'Not till after the clock had struck twelve, and I'd eaten all my bread and cheese,' said Mr Wray, rather piteously. 'I was glad enough when I heard the church door open at last, from the vestry where I had popped in but a moment before. It was the same woman came in who had shown the bust in the afternoon. I waited my time; and then slipped into the church; but she turned round sharply, just as I'd got halfway out, and came up to me. I never was frightened by an old woman before; but I can tell you, *she* frightened me. "Oh! there you are again!" says she: "Come, I say! this won't do. You sneaked out yesterday afternoon without paying anything; and you sneak in again after me, as soon as I open the door this morning – ain't you ashamed of being so shabby as that, at your age? – ain't you?" I never paid money in my life, Annie, with pleasure, till I gave that old woman some to stop her mouth! And I don't recollect either that I'd ever tried to run since leaving the stage (where we had a good deal of running, first and last, in the battle scenes); but I ran as soon as I got well away from the church, I can promise you – ran almost the whole way home.'

'That's what made you look so tired when you came in, grandfather,' said Annie; 'we couldn't think what was the matter with you at the time.'

'Well,' continued the old man, 'as soon as I could possibly get away from you, after coming back, I went and locked myself into my bedroom, pulled the mould in a great hurry out of the canvas bag, and took the cast at once – a beautiful cast! a perfect cast! I never produced a better when I was in good practice, Annie! When I sat down on the side of the bed, and looked at Shakspeare – *my* Shakspeare – got with so much danger, and made with my own hands – so white and pure and beautiful, just out of the mould! Old as I am, it was all I could do to keep myself from dancing for joy!'

'And yet, grandfather,' said Annie reproachfully, 'you could keep all that joy to yourself: you could keep it from *me!*'

'It was wrong my love, wrong on my part not to trust you – I'm sorry for it now. But the joy, after all, lasted a very little while – only from the afternoon to the evening. In the evening, if you remember, I went out to the butcher's to buy something for my own supper; something I could fancy, to make me comfortable before I went to bed (you little thought how I wanted my bed that night!) Well, when I got into the shop, several people were there; and what do you think they were all talking about? It makes me shudder even to remember it now! They were talking about a cast having been taken – *feloniously* taken, just fancy that, from the Stratford bust!'

Annie looked pale again instantly at this part of the story. As for 'Julius Caesar,' though he said nothing, he was evidently suffering from a second attack of the sympathetic cold perspiration which had already troubled him. He used the cotton handkerchief more copiously than ever just at this moment.

'The butcher was speaking when I came in,' pursued Mr Wray. '"Who's been and took it," says the fellow, (his grammer and elocution were awful, Annie!) "nobody don't know yet; but the Town Council will know by to-morrow, and then he'll be took himself." "Ah," says a dirty little man in black, "he'll be cast into prison, for taking a cast – eh?" They laughed, actually laughed at this vile pun. Then another man asked how it had been found out. "Some says," answered the butcher, "he was seen a doin' of it, through the window, by some chap looking in accidental like: some says, nobody don't know but the churchwardens, and *they* won't tell till they've got him." "Well," says a woman, waiting with a basket to be served, "but how will they get him? – (two chops, please, when you're quite ready) – that's the thing: how will they get him?" "Quite easy; take my word for it;" says the man who made the bad pun. "In the first place, they've posted up hand-bills, offering a reward for him; in the second place, they're going to examine the people who show the church; in the third place——" "Bother your places!" cried the woman, "I wish I could get my chops." "There you are, Mum," says the butcher, cutting of the chops, "and if you want my opinion about this business, it's this here: they'll transport him right away, in no time." "They can't," cries the dirty man, 'they can only imprison him."

"For life – eh?" says the woman, going off with the chops. "Be so kind as
to let me have a couple of kidneys," said I; for my knees knocked
together, and I could stand it no longer'

'Then you thought, grandfather, that they suspected you?'

'I thought everything that was horrible, Annie. However, I got my
kidneys, and went out unhindered, leaving them still talking about it. On
my way home I saw the hand-bill – the hand-bill itself! Ten pounds
reward for apprehending the man who had taken the cast! I read it twice
through, in a sort of trance of terror. My mask taken away, and myself put
in prison, if not transported – that was the prospect I had to give me an
appetite for the kidneys. There was only one thing to be done: to get
away from Stratford while I had the chance. The night-coach went that
very evening, straight through to this place, which was far enough off for
safety. We had some money, you know, left, after that last private-
theatrical party, where they treated us so generously. In short, I made you
pack up, Annie, as you said just now, and got you both off by the coach,
in time, not daring to speak a word about my secret, and as miserable as I
could be the whole journey. But let us say no more about that – here we
are, safe and sound! and here's my face of Shakspeare – my diamond
above all price – safe and sound, too! You shall see it; you shall look at
the mask, both of you, and then, I hope, you'll acknowledge that you
know as much as I do, about the mystery!'

'But, the mould,' cried Annie; 'hav'nt you got the mould with you,
too?'

'Lord bless my soul!' exclaimed Mr Wray, slapping both hands, in
desperation, on the lid of the cash-box. 'Between the fright and the
hurry of getting away, I quite forgot it – it's left at Stratford!'

'Left at Stratford!' echoed Annie, with a vague feeling of dismay, that
she could not account for.

'Yes: rolled up in the canvas bag, and poked behind the landlord's
volumes of the "Annual Register," on the top shelf of the cupboard, in
my bedroom. Between thinking of how to take care of the mask, and
how to take care of myself, I quite forgot it. Don't look so frightened,
Annie! The people at the lodgings are not likely to find it; and if they
did, they woudn't know what it was, and would throw it away. I've got
the mask; and that's all I want – the mould is of no consequence to *me*,
now – it's the mask that's everything – everything in the world!'

'I can't help feeling frightened, grandfather; and I can't help wishing
you had brought away the mould, though I don't know why.'

'You're frightened, Annie, about the Stratford people coming after me
here – that's what you're frightened about. But, if you and Julius Caesar
keep the secret from everybody – and I know you will – there is no fear
at all. They won't catch me back at Stratford again, or you either; and if

the churchwardens themselves found the mould, *that* wouldn't tell them where I was gone, would it? Look up, you silly little Annie! We're quite safe here. Look up, and see the great sight I'm going to show you – a sight that nobody in England can show, but me; – the mask! the mask of Shakspeare!'

His cheeks flushed, his fingers trembled, as he took a key out of his pocket and put it into the lock of the old cash-box. 'Julius Caesar,' breathless with wonder and suspense, clapped both his hands behind him, to make sure of breaking nothing this time. Even Annie caught the infection of the old man's triumph and delight, and breathed quicker than usual when she heard the click of the opening lock.

'There!' cried Mr Wray, throwing back the lid; 'there is the face of William Shakspeare! there is the treasure which the greatest lord in this land doesn't possess – a copy of the Stratford bust! Look at the forehead! Who's got such a forehead now? Look at his eyes; look at his nose. He was not only the greatest man that ever lived, but the handsomest, too! Who says this isn't just what his face was; his face taken after death? Who's bold enough to say so? Just look at the mouth, dropped and open – that's one proof? Look at the cheek, under the right eye; don't you see a little paralytic gathering up of the muscle, not visible on the other side? – that's another proof! Oh, Annie! Annie! there's the very face that once looked out, alive and beaming, on this poor old world of ours! There's the man who's comforted me, informed me, made me what I am! There's the "counterfeit presentment," the precious earthly relic of that great spirit who is now with the angels in Heaven, and singing among the sweetest of them!'

His voice grew faint, and his eyes moistened. He stood looking on the mask, with a rapture and a triumph which no speech could express. At such moments as those, even through that poor, meagre face, the immortal spirit within could still shine out in the beauty which never dies! – even in that frail old earthly tenement, could still vindicate outwardly the divine destiny of all mankind!

They were yet gathered silently round the Shakspeare cast, when a loud knock sounded at the room door. Instantly, old Reuben banged down the lid of the cash-box, and locked it; and *as* instantly, without waiting for permission to enter, a stranger walked in.

He was dressed in a long great-coat, wore a red comforter round his neck, and carried a very old and ill-looking cat-skin cap in his hand. His face was uncommonly dirty; his eyes uncommonly inquisitive; his whiskers uncommonly plentiful; and his voice most uncommonly and determinately gruff, in spite of his efforts to dulcify it for the occasion.

'Miss, and gentlemen both, beggin' all your pardons,' said this new arrival, 'vich *is* Mr Wray?' As he spoke, his eyes travelled all round the room, seeing everything and everybody in it; and then glancing sharply at the cash-box.

'I am Mr Wray, sir,' exclaimed our old friend, considerably startled, but recovering the Kemble manner and the Kemble elocution as if by magic.

'Wery good,' said the stranger. 'Then, beggin' your pardon again, sir, in pertickler, could you be so kind as to 'blige me with a card o' terms? It's for a young gentleman as wants you, Mr Wray,' he continued in a whisper, approaching the old man, and quite abstractedly leaning one hand on the cash-box.

'Take your hand off that box, sir,' cried Mr Wray, in a very fierce manner, but with a very trembling voice. At the same moment, 'Julius Caesar' advanced a step or two, partially doubling his fist. The man with the cat-skin cap had probably never before been so nearly knocked down in his life. Perhaps he suspected as much; for he took his hand off the box in a great hurry.

'It was inadwertent, sir,' he remarked in explanation – 'a little inadwertency of mine, that's all. But *could* you 'blige me vith that card o' terms? The young gentleman as wants it has heerd of your advertisement; and, bein' d'awful shaky in his pronounciashun, as vell as 'scruciatin' bad at readin' aloud, he's 'ard up for improvement – the sort o' secret thing you gives, you know, to the oraytors and the clujjymen, at three-and-six an hour. You'll heer from him in secret, Mr Wray, sir; and precious vork you'll 'ave to git him to rights; but do just 'blige me vith the card o' terms and the number of the 'ouse; 'cos I promised to git 'em for him today.'

'There is a card, sir, and I will engage to improve his delivery be it ever so bad,' said Mr Wray, considerably relieved at hearing the real nature of the stranger's errand.

'Miss, and gentlemen both, good mornin',' said the man, putting on his cat-skin cap, 'you'll heer from the young gentleman to-day; and wotever you do, sir, mind you keep the h'applicashun a secret – mind that!' He winked; and went out.

'I declare,' muttered Mr Wray, as the door closed, 'I thought he was a thief-taker from Stratford. Think of his being only a messenger from a new pupil! I told you we should have a pupil to-day. I told you so.'

'A very strange-looking messenger, grandfather, for a young gentleman to choose!' said Annie.

'He can't help his looks, my dear; and I'm sure we shan't mind them, if he brings us money. Have you seen enough of the mask? if you haven't I'll open the box again.'

'Enough for to-day, I think, grandfather. But, tell me, why do you keep the mask in that old cash-box?'

'Because I've nothing else, Annie, that will hold it, and lock up too. I was sorry, my dear, to disturb your 'odds and ends,' as you call them; but really there was nothing else to take. Stop! I've a thought! Julius Caesar shall make me a new box for the mask, and then you shall have your old one back again.'

'I don't want it, grandfather! I'd rather we none of us had it. Carrying a cash-box like that about with us, might make some people think we had money in it.'

'Money! People think *I* have any money! Come, come, Annie! that really won't do! That's much too good a joke, you sly little puss, you!;' And the old man laughed heartily, as he hurried off, to deposit the precious mask in his bedroom.

'You'll make that new box, Julius Caesar, won't you?' said Annie earnestly, as soon as her grandfather left the room.

'I'll get some wood, this very day,' answered the carpenter, 'and turn out such a box, by to-morrow, as – as——' He was weak at comparisons; so he stopped at the second 'as.'

'Make it quick, dear, make it quick,' said the little girl, anxiously; 'and then we'll give away the old cash-box. If grandfather had only told us what he was going to do, at first, he need never have used it; for you could have made him a new box beforehand. But, never mind! make it quick, now!'

Oh, 'Julius Caesar!' strictly obey your little betrothed in this, as in all other injunctions! You know now how soon that new box may be needed, or how much evil it may yet prevent!

CHAPTER V

CHUMMY DICK

Perhaps, by this time, you are getting tired of three such simple, homely characters as Mr and Miss Wray, and Mr 'Julius Caesar,' the carpenter. I strongly suspect you, indeed, of being downright anxious to have a little literary stimulant provided in the shape of a villain. You shall taste this stimulant – double distilled; for I have *two* villains all ready for you in the present chapter.

But, take my word for it, when you know your new company, you will be only too glad to get back again to Mr Wray and his family.

About three miles from Tidbury-on-the-Marsh, there is a village called Little London; sometimes, popularly entitled, in allusion to the characters frequenting it, 'Hell-End.' It is a dirty, ruinous-looking collection of some dozen cottages, and an ale-house. Ruffianly men, squalid women, filthy children, are its inhabitants. The chief support of this pleasant population is currently supposed to be derived from their connection with the poaching and petty larcenous interests of their native soil. In a word, Little London looks bad, smells bad, and *is* bad; a fouler blot of a village, in the midst of a prettier surrounding landscape, is not to be found in all England.

Our principal business is with the ale-house. The 'Jolly Ploughboys' is the sign; and Judith Grimes, widow, is the proprietor. The less said about Mrs Grimes's character, the better; it is not quite adapted to bear discussion in these pages. Mrs Grimes's mother (who is now bordering on eighty) may be also dismissed to merciful oblivion; for, at her daughter's age, she was − if possible − rather the worse of the two. Towards her son, Mr Benjamin Grimes (as one of the rougher sex), I feel less inclined to be compassionate. When I assert that he was in every respect a complete specimen of a provincial scoundrel, I am guilty, according to a profound and reasonable maxim of our law, of uttering a great libel, because I am repeating a great truth.

You know the sort of man well. You have seen the great, hulking, heavy-browed, sallow-complexioned fellow often enough, lounging at village corners, with a straw in his mouth and a bludgeon in his hand. Perhaps you have asked your way of him; and have been answered by a growl and a petition for money; or, you have heard of him in connection with a cowardly assault on your rural policeman; or a murderous fight with your friend's game-keeper; or a bad case for your other friend, the magistrate, at petty sessions. Anybody who has ever been in the country, knows the man − the ineradicable plague-spot of his whole neighbourhood − as well as I do.

About eight o'clock in the evening, and on the same day which had been signalised by Mr Wray's disclosures, Mrs Grimes, senior, − or, as she was generally called, 'Mother Grimes,' − sat in her arm-chair in the private parlour of The Jolly Ploughboys, just making up her mind to go to bed. Her ideas on this subject rather wanted acceleration; and they got it from her dutiful son, Mr Benjamin Grimes.

'Coom, old 'ooman, why does'nt thee trot up stairs?' demanded this provincial worthy.

'I'm a-going, Ben, − gently, Judith! − I'm a-going!' mumbled the old woman, as Mrs Grimes, junior, entered the room, and very unceremoniously led her mother off.

'Mind thee doesn't let nobody in here to-night,' bawled Benjamin, as his sister went out. 'Chummy Dick's going to coom,' he added, in a mysterious whisper.

Left to himself to await the arrival of Chummy Dick, Mr Grimes found time hang rather heavy on his hands. He first looked out of the window. The view commanded a few cottages and fields, with a wood beyond on the rising ground, – a homely scene enough in itself; but the heavenly purity of the shining moonlight gave it, just now, a beauty not its own. This beauty was not apparently to the taste of Mr Grimes, for he quickly looked away from the window back into the room. Staring dreamily, his sunken sinister grey eyes fixed upon the opposite wall, encountering there nothing but four coloured prints, representing the career of the prodigal son. He had seen them hundreds of times before; but he looked at them again from mere habit.

In the first of the series, the prodigal son was clothed in a bright red dress coat, and was just getting on horseback (the wrong side); while his father, in a bright blue coat, helped him on with one hand, and pointed disconsolately with the other to a cheese-coloured road, leading straight from the horse's fore-feet to a distant city in the horizon, entirely composed of towers. In the second plate, master prodigal was feasting between two genteel ladies, holding gold wine-glasses in their hands; while a debauched companion sprawled on the ground by his side, in a state of cataleptic drunkenness. In the third, he lay on his back; his red coat torn, and showing his purple skin; one of his stockings off; a thunderstorm raging over his head, and two white sows standing on either side of him – one of them apparently feeding off the calf of his leg. In the fourth——

Just as Mr Grimes had got to the fourth print he heard somebody whistling a tune outside, and turned to the window. It was Chummy Dick; or, in other words the man with the cat-skin cap, who had honoured Mr Wray with a morning call.

Chummy Dick's conduct on entering the parlour had the merit of originality as an exhibition of manners. He took no more notice of Mr Grimes than if he had not been in the room; drew his chair to the fire-place; put one foot on each of the hobs; pulled a little card out of his great-coat pocket; read it; and then indulged himself in a long, steady, unctuous fit of laughter, cautiously pitched in what musicians would call the 'minor key.'

'What dost thee laugh about like that?' asked Grimes.

'Git a glass of 'ot grog fust – two lumps o' sugar, mind! – and then, Benjamin, you'll know in no time!' said Chummy Dick, maintaining an undercurrent of laughter all the while he spoke.

While Benjamin is gone for the grog, there is time enough for a word or two of explanation.

Possibly you may remember that the young assistant at Messrs Dunball and Dark's happened to see Mr Wray carrying his cash-box into No. 12. The same gust of wind which, by blowing aside old Reuben's cloak, betrayed what he had got under it to this assistant, exposed the same thing, at the same time, to the observation of Mr Grimes, who happened to be lounging about the High Street on the occasion in question. Knowing nothing about either the mask or the mystery connected with it, it was only natural that Benjamin should consider the cash-box to be a receptacle for cash; and it was, furthermore, not at all out of character that he should ardently long to be possessed of that same cash, and should communicate his desire to Chummy Dick.

And for this reason. With all the ambition to be a rascal of first-rate ability, Mr Grimes did not possess the necessary cunning and capacity, and had not received the early London education requisite to fit him for so exalted a position. Stealing poultry out of a farm-yard, for instance, was quite in Benjamin's line; but stealing a cash-box out of a barred and bolted-up house, standing in the middle of a large town, was an achievement above his powers – an achievement that but one man in his circle of acquaintance was mighty enough to compass – and that man was Chummy Dick, the great London house-breaker. Certain recent passages in the life of this illustrious personage had rendered London and its neighbourhood very insecure, in his case, for purposes of residence, so he had retired to a safe distance in the provinces; and had selected Tidbury and the adjacent country as a suitable field for action, and a very pretty refuge from the Bow-street Runners into the bargain.

'Wery good, Benjamin; and not too sveet,' remarked Chummy Dick, tasting the grog which Grimes had brought him. He was not, by any means, one of your ferocious house-breakers, except under strong provocation. There was more of oil than of aqua-fortis in the mixture of his temperament. His robberies were marvels of skill, cunning, and cool determination. In short, he stole plate or money out of dwelling-houses, as cats steal cream off breakfast-tables – by biding his time, and never making a noise.

'Hast thee seen the cash-box?' asked Grimes, in an eager whisper.

'Look at my 'and, Benjamin,' was the serenely triumphant answer. 'It's bin on the cash-box! You're all right: the swag's ready for us.'

'Swag! Wot be that?'

'That's swag!' said Chummy Dick, pulling half-a-crown out of his pocket, and solemnly holding it up for Benjamin's inspection. 'I havn't got a fi' pun' note, or a christenin' mug about me; but notes and silver's swag, too. Now, young Grimes, you knows swag; and you'll *have* your swag before long, if you looks out sharp. If it ain't quite so fine a night to-morrer – if there ain't quite so much of that moonshine as there is now to let gratis for nothin' – why, we'll 'ave the cash-box!'

'Half on it for *me*! Thee knows't that, Chummy Dick!'

'Check that ere talky-talky tongue of your'n; and you'll 'ave your 'alf. I've bin to see the old man; and he's gived me his wistin' card, with the number of the 'ouse. Ho! ho! ho! think of his givin' his card to *me*! It's as good as inwitin' one to break into the 'ouse – it is, every bit!' And, with another explosion of laughter, Chummy Dick triumphantly threw Mr Wray's card into the fire.

'But that ain't the *pint*,' he resumed, when he had recovered his breath. 'We'll stick to the pint – the pins's the cash-box.' And, to do him justice, he *did* stick to the point, never straying away from it, by so much as a hair's breadth, for a full half-hour.

The upshot of the long harangue to which he now treated Mr Benjamin Grimes, was briefly this: he had invented a plan, after reading the old man's advertisement first, for getting into Mr Wray's lodgings unsuspected; he had seen the cash-box with his own eyes, and was satisfied, from certain indications, that there was money in it – he held the owner of this property to be a miser, whose gains were all hoarded up in his cash-box, stray shillings and stray sovereigns together – he had next found out who were the inmates of the house; and had discovered that the only formidable person sleeping at No. 12 was our friend the carpenter – he had then examined the premises; and had seen that they were easily accessible by the back drawing-room window, which looked out on the wash-house roof – finally, he had ascertained that the two watchmen appointed to guard the town, performed that duty by going to bed regularly at eleven o'clock, and leaving the town to guard itself; the whole affair was perfectly easy – too easy in fact for any body but a young beginner.

'Now, Benjamin,' said Chummy Dick, in conclusion – 'mind this: no wiolence! Take your swag quiet, and you takes it safe. Wiolence is sometimes as bad as knockin' up a whole street – wiolence is the downy cracksman's last kick-out when he's caught in a fix. Fust and foremost, you've got your mask,' (here he pulled out a shabby domino mask,) 'wery good; nobody can't swear to you in that. Then, you've got your barker,' (he produced a pistol,) 'just to keep 'em quiet with the look of it, and if that wont do, there's your gag and bit o' rope' (he drew them forth,) 'for their mouths and 'ands. Never pull your trigger, till you see another man ready to pull his. Then you *must* make your row; and then you make it to some purpose. The nobs in our business – remember this, young Grimes! – always takes the swag easy; and when they can't take it easy, they takes it as easy as they can. That's wisdom – the wisdom of life!'

'Why thee bean't a-going, man?' asked Benjamin in astonishment, as the philosophical housebreaker abruptly moved towards the door.

'Me and you mustn't be seen together, to-morrer,' said Chummy Dick, in a whisper. 'You let me alone: I've got business to do to-night – never mind wot! At eleven to-morrer night, you be at the cross roads that meets on the top of the common. Look out sharp; and you'll see *me*.'

'But if so be it do keep moonshiny,' suggested Grimes.

'On second thoughts, Benjamin,' said the housebreaker, after a moment's reflection, 'we'll risk all the moonshine as ever shone – High Street, Tidbury, ain't Bow-street, London! – we may risk it safe. Moon, or no moon, young Grimes! to-morrer night's *our* night!'

By this time he had walked out of the house. They separated at the door. The radiant moonlight falling lovely on all things, fell lovely even on *them*. How pure it was! how doubly pure, to shine on Benjamin Grimes and Chummy Dick, and not be soiled by the contact!

CHAPTER VI

A MORNING VISIT

During the whole remainder of Annie's birthday, Mr Wray sat at home, anxiously expecting the promised communication from the mysterious new pupil whose elocution wanted so much setting to rights. Though he never came, and never wrote, old Reuben still persisted in expecting him forthwith; and still waited for him as patiently the next morning, as he had waited the day before.

Annie sat in the room with her grandfather, occupied in making lace. She had learnt this art, so as to render herself, if possible, of some little use in contributing to the general support; and, sometimes, her manufacture actually poured a few extra shillings into the scantily-filled family coffer. Her lace was not at all the sort of thing that your fine people would care to look at twice – it was just simple and pretty, like herself; and only sold (when it *did* sell, and that alas! was not often!) among ladies whose purses were very little better furnished than her own.

'Julius Caesar' was down stairs, in the back kitchen, making the all-important box – or, as the landlady irritably phrased it, 'making a mess about the house.' She was not partial to sawdust and shavings, and almost lost her temper when the gluepot invaded the kitchen fire. But work away, honest carpenter! work away, and never mind her! Get the mask of Shakspeare out of the old box, and into the new, before night comes; and you will have done the best day's work you ever completed in your life!

Annie and her grandfather had a great deal of talk about the Shakspeare cast, while they were sitting together in the drawing-room. If I were to report all old Reuben's rhapsodies and quotations during that period, I might fill the whole remaining space accorded to me in this little book. It was only once that the conversation varied at all. Annie just asked, by way of changing the subject a little, how a plaster cast was taken from the mould; and Mr Wray instantly went off at a tangent, in the midst of a new quotation, to tell her. He was still describing, for the second time, how the plaster and water were to be mixed, how the mixture was to be left to 'set,' and how the mould was to be pulled off it, when the landlady, looking very hot and important, bustled into the room, exclaiming:–

'Mr Wray, sir! Mr Wray! Here's Squire Colebatch, of Cropley Court, coming upstairs to see you!' She then added, in a whisper: 'He's very hot-tempered and odd, sir, but the best gentleman in the world——'

'That will do, ma'am! that will do!' interrupted a hearty voice, outside the door. 'I can introduce myself; an old play-writer and an old play-actor don't want much introduction, I fancy! How are you, Mr Wray? I've come to make your acquaintance: how do you do, sir!'

Before the Squire came in, Mr Wray's first idea was that the young gentleman pupil had arrived at last – but when the Squire appeared, he discovered that he was mistaken. Mr Colebatch was an old gentleman with a very rosy face, with bright black eyes that twinkled incessantly, and with perfectly white hair, growing straight up from his head in a complete forest of venerable bristles. Moreover, his elocution wanted no improvement at all; and his 'delivery' proclaimed itself at once, as the delivery of a gentleman – a very eccentric one, but a gentleman still.

'Now, Mr Wray,' said the Squire, sitting down, and throwing open his great-coat, with the air of an old friend; 'I've a habit of speaking to the point, because I hate ceremony and botheration. My name's Matthew Colebatch; I live at Cropley Court, just outside the town; and I come to see you, because I've had an argument about your character with the Reverend Daubeny Daker, the Rector here!'

Astonishment bereft Mr Wray of all power of speech, while he listened to this introductory address.

'I'll tell you how it was, sir,' continued the Squire. 'In the first place, Daubeny Daker's a canting sneak – a sort of fellow who goes into poor people's cottages, asking what they've got for dinner, and when they tell him, he takes the cover off the saucepan and sniffs at it, to make sure that they've spoken the truth. That's what *he* calls doing his duty to the poor, and what *I* call being a canting sneak! Well, Daubeny Daker saw your advertisement in Dunball's shop window. I must tell you, by-the-by, that he calls theatres the devil's houses, and actors the devil's missionaries; I heard him say that in a sermon, and have never been into his church since! Well, sir, he read your advertisement; and when he came to that part about improving clergymen at three-and-sixpence an hour (it would be damned cheap to improve Daubeny Daker at that price!) he falls into one of his nasty, cold-blooded, sneering rages, goes into the shop, and insists on having the thing taken down, as an insult offered by a vagabond actor to the clerical character – don't lose your temper, Mr Wray, don't, for God's sake – I trounced him about it handsomely, I can promise you! And now, what do you think that fat jackass Dunball did, when he heard what the parson said? Took your card down! – took it out of the window directly, as if Daubeny Daker was King of Tidbury, and it was death to disobey him!'

'My character, sir!' interposed Mr Wray.

'Stop, Mr Wray! I beg your pardon; but I *must* tell you how I trounced him. Half an hour after the thing had been taken down, I dropped into the shop. Dunball, smiling like a fool, tells me about the business. "Put it up again, directly!" said I; "I won't have any man's character bowled down like that by people who don't know him!" Dunball makes a wry face and hesitates. I pull out my watch, and say to him, "I give you a minute to decide between *my* custom and interest, and Daubeny Daker's." I happen to be what's called a rich man, Mr Wray; so Dunball decided in about two seconds, and up went your advertisement again, just where it was before!'

'I have no words, sir, to thank you for your kindness,' said poor old Reuben.

'Hear how I trounced Daubeny Daker, sir – hear that! I met him out at dinner, the same night. He was talking about you, and what he'd done – as proud as a peacock! "In fact," says he, at the end of his speech, "I considered it my duty, as a clergyman, to have the advertisement taken down." "And I considered it my duty, as a gentleman," said I, "to have it put up again." *Then*, we began the argument (he hates me, because I once wrote a play – I know he does). I won't tell you what he said, because it would distress you. But it ended, after we'd been at it, hammer and tongs, for about an hour, by my saying that his conduct in setting you down as a disreputable character, without making a single enquiry about you, showed a want of Christianity, justice, and common sense. "I can bear with your infirmities of temper, Mr Colebatch," says he, in his nasty, sneering way; "but allow me to ask, do *you*, who defend Mr Wray so warmly, know any more of him than I do?" He thought this was a settler; but I was at him again, quick as lightning. "No, sir; but I'll set you a proper example, by going to-morrow morning, and judging of the man from the man himself!" That was a settler for *him*: and now, here I am this morning, to do what I said.'

'I will show you, Mr Colebatch, that I have deserved the honour of being defended by you,' said Mr Wray, with a mixture of artless dignity and manly gratitude in his manner, which became him wonderfully; 'I have a letter, sir, from the late Mr Kemble——'

'What, my old friend, John Philip!' cried the Squire; 'let's see it instantly! He, Mr Wray, was "the noblest Roman of them all,' as Shakspeare says."

Here was an inestimable friend indeed! He knew Mr Kemble and quoted Shakspeare. Old Reuben could actually have embraced the Squire at that moment; but he contented himself with producing the great Kemble letter.

Mr Colebatch read it, and instantly declared, that, as a certificate of character, it beat all other certificates that ever were written completely out of the field; and established Mr Wray's reputation as above the reach of all calumny. 'It's the most tremendous crusher for Daubeny Daker that ever was composed, sir!' Just as the old gentleman said this, his eyes encountered little Annie, who had been sitting quietly in the corner of the room, going on with her lace. He had hardly allowed himself leisure enough to look at her, in the first heat of his introductory address, but he made up for lost time now, with characteristic celerity.

'Who's that pretty little girl?' said he; and his bright eyes twinkled more than ever as he spoke.

'My grand-daughter, Annie,' answered Mr Wray, proudly.

'Nice little thing! how pretty and quiet she sits making her lace!' cried Mr Colebatch, enthusiastically. 'Don't move, Annie; don't go away! I like to look at you! You won't mind a queer old bachelor, like me – will you? You'll let me look at you, won't you? Go on with your lace, my dear, and Mr Wray and I will go on with our chat.'

This 'chat' completed what the Kemble letter had begun. Encouraged by the Squire, old Reuben artlessly told the little story of his life, as if to an intimate friend; and told it with all the matchless pathos of simplicity and truth. What time Mr Colebatch could spare from looking at Annie – and that was not much – he devoted to anathematising his implacable enemy, Daubeny Daker, in a series of violent expletives; and anticipating, with immense glee, the sort of consummate 'trouncing' he should now be able to inflict on that reverend gentleman, the next time he met with him. Mr Wray only wanted to take one step more after this in the Squire's estimation, to be considered the phoenix of all professors of elocution, past, present, and future: and he took it. He actually recollected the production of Mr Colebatch's play – a tragedy all bombast and bloodshed – at Drury Lane Theatre; and, more than that, he had himself performed one of the minor characters in it!

The Squire seized his hand immediately. This play (in virtue of which he considered himself a dramatic author,) was his weak point. It had enjoyed a very interrupted 'run' of one night; and had never been heard of after. Mr Colebatch attributed this circumstance entirely to public misappreciation; and, in his old age, boasted of his tragedy wherever he went, utterly regardless of the reception it had met with. It has often been asserted that the parents of sickly children are the parents who love their children best. This remark is sometimes, and only sometimes, true. Transfer it, however, to the sickly children of literature, and it directly becomes a rule which the experience of the whole world is powerless to confute by a single exception!

'My dear sir!' cried Mr Colebatch, 'your remembrance of my play is a new bond between us! It was entitled – of course you recollect – 'The Mysterious Murderess.' Gad, sir, do you happen to call to mind the last four lines of the guilty Lindamira's death-scene? It ran thus, Mr Wray:–

'Murder and midnight hail! Come all he horrors!
My soul's congenial darkness quite defies ye!
I'm sick with guilt! – What is to cure me? – This! (*Stabs herself.*)
Ha! ha! I'm better now – (*smiles faintly*) – I'm comfortable!' (*Dies*).

'If that's not pretty strong writing, sir, my name's not Matthew Colebatch! and yet the besotted audience failed to appreciate it! Bless my soul!' (pulling out his watch) 'one o'clock, already! I ought to be at home! I must go directly. Good-bye, Mr Wray. I'm so glad to have seen you, that I could almost thank Daubeny Daker for putting me in the towering passion that sent me here. You remind me of my young days, when I used to go behind the scenes, and sup with Kemble and Matthews. Good-bye, little Annie! I'm a wicked old fellow, and I mean to kiss you some day! Not a step further, Mr Wray; not a step, by George, sir; or I'll never come again. I mean to make the Tidbury people employ your talents; they're the most infernal set of asses under the canopy of heaven; but they *shall* employ them! I engage you to read my play, if nothing else will do, at the Mechanics' Institution. We'll make their flesh creep, sir; and their hair stand on end, with a little tragedy of the good old school. Good-bye, till I see you again, and God bless you!' And away the talkative old squire went, in a mighty hurry, just as he had come in.'

'Oh, grandfather! what a nice old gentleman!' exclaimed Annie, looking up for the first time from her lace-cushion.

'What unexampled kindess to *me!* What perfect taste in everything! Did you hear him quote Shakspeare?' cried old Reuben, in an ecstasy. They went on alternately, in this way, with raptures about Mr Colebatch, for something like an hour. After that time, Annie left her work, and walked to the window.

'It's raining – raining fast,' she said. 'Oh, dear me! we can't have our walk to-day!'

'Hark! there's the wind moaning,' said the old man. 'It's getting colder, too. Annie! we are going to have a stormy night.'

* * *

Four o'clock! And the carpenter still at his work in the back kitchen. Faster, 'Julius Caesar,' faster. Let us have that mask of Shakspeare out of Mr Wray's cash-box, and snugly ensconced in your neat wooden casket, before anybody goes to bed to-night. Faster, man! – Faster!

CHAPTER VII

A NIGHT VISIT

For some household reason not worth mentioning, they dined later that day than usual at No. 12. It was five o'clock before they sat down to table. The conversation all turned on the visitor of the morning; no terms in Mr Wray's own vocabulary being anything like choice enough to characterise the eccentric old squire, he helped himself to Shakspeare, even more largely than usual, every time he spoke of Mr Colebatch. He managed to discover some striking resemblance to that excellent gentleman (now in one particular, and now in another), in every noble and venerable character, throughout the whole series of the plays – not forgetting either, on one or two occasions, to trace the corresponding likeness between the more disreputable and intriguing personages, and that vindictive enemy to all plays, players, and play-houses, the Reverend Daubeny Daker. Never did any professed commentator on Shakspeare (and the assertion is a bold one) wrest the poet's mighty meaning more dexterously into harmony with his own microscopic ideas, than Mr Wray now wrested it, to furnish him with eulogies on the goodness and generosity of Mr Matthew Colebatch, of Cropley Court.

Meanwhile, the weather got worse and worse, as the evening advanced. The wind freshened almost to a gale; and dashed the fast-falling rain against the window, from time to time, with startling violence. It promised to be one of the wildest, wettest, darkest nights they had had at Tidbury since the winter began.

Shortly after the table was cleared, having pretty well exhausted himself on the subject of Mr Colebatch, for the present, old Reuben fell asleep in his chair. This was rather an unusual indulgence for him, and was probably produced by the especial lateness of the dinner. Mr Wray generally took that meal at two o'clock, and set off for his walk afterwards, reckless of all the ceremonial observances of digestion. He was a poor man, and could not afford the luxurious distinction of being dyspeptic.

The behaviour of Mr 'Julius Caesar,' the carpenter, when he appeared from the back kitchen to take his place at dinner, was rather perplexing. He knocked down a salt-cellar; spirted some gravy over his shirt; and spilt a potato, in trying to transport it a distance of about four inches, from the dish to Annie's plate. This, to begin with, was rather above the general average of his number of table accidents at one meal. Then, when dinner was over, he announced his intention of returning to the back kitchen for the rest of the evening, in tones of such unwonted mystery, that Annie's curiosity was aroused, and she began to question him. Had he not done the new box yet? No! Why, he might have made such a box in an hour, surely? Yes, he might. And why had he not? 'Wait a bit, Annie, and you'll see!' And having said that, he laid his large finger mysteriously against the side of his large nose, and walked out of the room forthwith.

In half-an-hour afterwards he came in again, looking very sheepish and discomposed, and trying, unsuccessfully, to hide an enormous poultice – a perfect loaf of warm bread and water – which decorated the palm of his right hand. This time, Annie insisted on an explanation.

It appeared that he had conceived the idea of ornamenting the lid of the new box with some uncouth carvings of his own, in compliment to Mr Wray and the mask of Shakspeare. Being utterly unpractised in the difficult handiwork he proposed to perform, he had run a splinter into the palm of his hand. And there the box was now in the back kitchen, waiting for lock and hinges, while the only person in the house who could put them on, was not likely to handle a hammer again for days to come. Miserable 'Julius Caesar!' Never was well-meant attention more fatally misdirected than this attention of yours! Of all the multifarious accidents of your essentially accidental life, this special casualty, which has hindered you from finishing the new box to-night, is the most ill-timed and the most irreparable!

When the tea came in Mr Wray woke up; and as it usually happens with people who seldom indulge in the innocent sensuality of an after-dinner nap, changed at once, from a state of extreme somnolence to a state of extreme wakefulness. By this time the night was at its blackest; the rain fell fierce and thick, and the wild wind walked abroad in the darkness, in all its might and glory. The storm began to affect Annie's spirits a little, and she hinted as much to her grandfather, when he awoke. Old Reuben's extraordinary vivacity immediately suggested a remedy for this. He proposed to read a play of Shakspeare's, as the surest mode of diverting attention from the weather; and, without allowing a moment for the consideration of his offer, he threw open the book, and began 'Macbeth.'

As he not only treated his hearers to every one of the Kemble pauses, and every infinitesimal inflection of the Kemble elocution, throughout the reading; but also exhibited a serious parody of Mrs Siddons' effects in Lady Macbeth's sleep-walking scene, with the aid of a white pocket-handkerchief, tied under his chin, and a japanned bed-room-candlestick in his hand – and as, in addition to these special and strictly dramatic delays, he further hindered the progress of his occupation by vigilantly keeping his eye on 'Julius Caesar,' and unmercifully waking up that ill-starred carpenter every time he went to sleep, (which, by the way, was once in every ten minutes,) nobody can be surprised to hear that Macbeth was not finished before eleven o'clock. The hour was striking from Tidbury Church, as Mr Wray solemnly declaimed the last lines of the tragedy, and shut up the book.

'There!' said old Reuben, 'I think I've put the weather out of your head, Annie, by this time! You look sleepy, my dear; go to bed. I had a few remarks to make, about the right reading of Macbeth's dagger-scene, but I can make them to-morrow morning, just as well. I won't keep you up any longer. Good-night, love!'

Was Mr Wray not going to bed, too? No: he never felt more awake in his life; he would sit up a little, and have a good 'warm' over the fire. Should Annie bear him company? By no means! he would not keep poor Annie from her bed, on any account. Should 'Julius Caesar'? – Certainly not! he was sure to go to sleep immediately; and to hear him snore, Mr Wray said, was worse than hearing him sneeze. So the two young people wished the old man good-night, and left him to have his 'warm,' as he desired. This was the way in which he prepared himself to undergo that luxurious process:–

He drew his arm-chair in front of the fire, then put a chair on either side of it, then unlocked the cupboard, and took out the cash-box that contained the mask of Shakspeare. This he deposited upon one of the side chairs; and upon the other he put his copy of the Plays, and the candle. Finally, he sat down in the middle – cosy beyond all description – and slowly inhaled a copious pinch of snuff.

'How it blows, outside!' said old Reuben, 'and how snug I am, in here!'

He unlocked the cash-box, and taking it on his knee, looked down on the mask that lay inside. Gradually, the pride and pleasure at first appearing in his eyes, gave place to a dreamy fixed expression. He gently closed the lid, and reclined back in his chair; but he did not shut up the cash-box for the night, for he never turned the key in the lock.

Old recollections were crowding on him, revived by his conversation of the morning with Mr Colebatch; and now evoked by many a Shakspeare association of his own, always connected with the treasured, the inestimable mask. Tender remembrances spoke piteously and solemnly within him. Poor Columbine – lost, but never forgotten –

moved loveliest and holiest of all those memory-shadows, through the dim world of his waking visions. How little the grave can hide of us! The love that began before it, lasts after it. The sunlight to which our eyes looked, while it shone on earth, changes but to the star that guides our memories when it passes to heaven!

Hark! the church-clock chimes the quarters; each stroke sounds with the ghostly wildness of all bell-tones, when heard amid the tumult of a storm, but fails to startle old Reuben now. He is far away in other scenes; living again in other times. Twelve strikes; and then, when the clock-bell rings its long midnight peal, he rouses – he hears that.

The fire has died down to one, dull, red spot: he feels chilled; and sitting up in his chair, yawning, tries to summon resolution enough to rise and go up stairs to bed. His expression is just beginning to grow utterly listless and weary, when it suddenly alters. His eyes look eager again; his lips close firmly; his cheeks get pale all at once – he is listening.

He fancies that, when the wind blows in the loudest gusts, or when the rain dashes heaviest against the window, he hears a very faint, curious sound – sometimes like a scraping noise, sometimes like a tapping noise. But in what part of the house – or even whether outside or in – he cannot tell. In the calmer moments of the storm, he listens with especial attention to find this out; but it is always at that very time that he hears nothing.

It must be imagination. And yet, that imagination is so like a reality that it has made him shudder all over twice in the last minute.

Surely he hears that strange noise now! Why not get up, and go to the window, and listen if the faint tapping comes by any chance from outside, in front of the house? Something seems to keep him in his chair, perfectly motionless – something makes him afraid to turn his head, for fear of seeing a sight of horror close to his side –

Hush! it sounds again, plainer and plainer. And now it changes to a cracking noise – close by – at the shutter of the back drawing-room window.

What is that, sliding along the crack between the folding doors and the floor? – a light! – a light in that empty room which nobody uses. And now, a whisper – footsteps – the handle on the lock of the door moves –

'Help! Help! for God's sake! – Murder! Mur——'

Just as that cry for help passed the old man's lips, the two robbers, masked and armed, appeared in the room; and the next instant, Chummy Dick's gag was fast over his mouth.

He had the cash-box clasped tight to his breast. Mad with terror, his eyes glared like a dead-man's, while he struggled in the powerful arms that held him.

Grimes, unused to such scenes, was so petrified by astonishment at finding the old man out of bed, and the room lit up, that he stood with his pistol extended, staring helplessly through the eye-holes of his mask. Not so with his experienced leader. Chummy Dick's ears and eyes were as quick as his hands – the first informed him that Reuben's cry for help (skilfully as he had stifled it with the gag) had aroused some one in the house: the second instantly detected the cash-box, as Mr Wray clasped it to his breast.

'Put up your pop-gun, you precious yokel, you!' whispered the housebreaker fiercely. 'Look alive; and pull it out of his arms. Damn you! do it quick! they're awake, up stairs!'

It was not easy to 'do it quick.' Weak as he was, Reuben actually held his treasure with the convulsive strength of despair, against the athletic ruffian who was struggling to get it away. Furious at the resistance, Grimes exerted his whole force, and tore the box so savagely from the old man's grasp, that the mask of Shakspeare flew several feet away, through the open lid, before it fell, shattered into fragments on the floor.

For an instant, Grimes stood aghast at the sight of what the contents of the cash-box really were. Then frantic with the savage passions produced by the discovery, he rushed up to the fragments, and, with a horrible oath, stamped his heavy boot upon them, as if the very plaster could feel his vengeance. 'I'll kill him, if I swing for it!' cried the villain, turning on Mr Wray the next moment, and raising his horse-pistol by the barrel over the old man's head.

But, exactly at the same time, brave as his heroic namesake, 'Julius Caesar' burst into the room. In the heat of the moment, he struck at Grimes with his wounded hand. Dealt even under that disadvantage, the blow was heavy enough to hurl the fellow right across the room, till he dropped down against the opposite wall. But the triumph of the stout carpenter was a short one. Hardly a second after his adversary had fallen, he himself lay stunned on the floor by the pistol-butt of Chummy Dick.

Even the nerve of the London housebreaker deserted him, at the first discovery of the astounding self-deception of which he and his companion had been the victims. He only recovered his characteristic coolness and self-possession when the carpenter attacked Grimes. Then, true to his system of never making unnecessary noise, or wasting unnecessary powder, he hit 'Julius Caesar' just behind the ear, with unerring dexterity. The blow made no sound, and seemed to be inflicted by a mere turn of the wrist; but it was decisive – he had thoroughly stunned his man.

And now, the piercing screams of the landlady, from the bedroom floor, poured quicker and quicker into the street, through the opened window. They were mingled with the fainter cries of Annie, whom the good woman forcibly detained from going into danger down stairs. The female servant (the only other inmate of the house) rivalled her mistress in shrieking madly and incessantly for help, from the window of the garret above.

'The whole street will be up in a crack!' cried Chummy Dick, swearing at every third word he uttered, and hauling the partially-recovered Grimes into an erect position again, 'there's no swag to be got here! step out quick, young yokel, or you'll be nabbed!'

He pushed Grimes into the back drawing-room; hustled him over the window-sill on to the wash-house roof, leaving him to find his own way, how he could, to the ground; and then followed, with Mr Wray's watch and purse, and a brooch of Annie's that had been left on the chimney-piece, all gathered into his capacious great-coat pocket in a moment. They were not worth much as spoils; but the dexterity with which they were taken instantly with one hand, while he had Grimes to hold with the other; and the strength, coolness, and skill he displayed in managing the retreat, were worthy even of the reputation of Chummy Dick. Long before the two Tidbury watchmen had begun to think of a pursuit, the housebreaker and his companion were out of reach – even though the Bow-street runners themselves had been on the spot to give chase.

★ ★ ★

How long the old man has kept in that one position! – crouching down there in the corner of the room, without stirring a limb or uttering a word. He dropped on his knees at that place, when the robbers left him; and nothing has moved him from it since.

When Annie broke away from the landlady, and ran down stairs – he never stirred. When the long wail of agony burst from her lips, as she saw the dead-look of the brave man lying stunned on the floor – he never spoke. When the street-door was opened; and the crowd of terrified, half-dressed neighbours all rushed together into the house, shouting and trampling about, half panic-stricken at the news they heard – he never noticed a single soul. When the doctor was sent for; and, amid an awful hush of expectation, proceeded to restore the carpenter to his senses – even at that enthralling moment, he never looked up. It was only when the room was cleared again – when his grand-daughter came to his side, and, putting her arms round his neck, laid her cold cheek close to his – that he seemed to live at all. Then, he just heaved a heavy sigh; his head dropped down lower on his breast; and he shivered throughout his whole frame, as if some icy influence was freezing him to the heart.

All that long, long time he had been looking on one sight – the fragments of the mask of Shakspeare lying beneath him. And there he kept now – when they tried in their various methods to coax him away –

still crouching over them; just in the same position; just with the same hard, frightful look about his face that they had seen from the first.

Annie went and fetched the cash-box; and tremblingly put it down before him. The instant he saw it, his eyes began to flash. He pounced in a fury of haste upon the fragments of the mask, and huddled them all together into the box, with shaking hands, and quick panting breath. He picked up the least chip of plaster that the robber had ground under his boot; and strained his eyes to look for more, when not an atom more was left. At last, he locked the box, and caught it up tight to his breast; and then he let them raise him up, and lead him gently away from the place.

He never quitted hold of his box, while they got him into bed. Annie, and her lover, and the landlady, all sat up together in his room; and all, in different degrees, felt the same horrible foreboding about him, and shrank from communicating it to one another. Occasionally, they heard him beating his hands strangely on the lid of the box; but he never spoke; and, as far as they could discover, never slept.

The doctor had said he would be better when the daylight came. – Did the doctor really know what was the matter with him? – and had the doctor any suspicion that something precious had been badly injured that night, besides the mask of Shakspeare?

CHAPTER VIII

A THOUGHT OF ANNIE'S

By the next morning the news of the burglary had not only spread all through Tidbury, but all though the adjacent villages as well. The very first person who called at No. 12, to see how they did after the fright of the night before, was Mr Colebatch. The old gentleman's voice was heard louder than ever, as he ascended the stairs with the landlady. He declared he would have both the Tidbury watchmen turned off, as totally unfit to take care of the town. He swore that, if it cost him a hundred pounds, he would fetch the Bow-street runners down from London, and procure the catching, trying, convicting, and hanging of 'those two infernal housebreakers' before Christmas came. Invoking vengeance and retribution in this way, at every fresh stair, the Squire's temperament was up at 'bloodheat,' by the time he got into the drawing-room. It fell directly, however, to 'temperate' again, when he found nobody there; and it sank twenty degrees lower still, at the sight of little Annie's face, when she came down to see him.

'Cheer up, Annie!' said the old gentleman, with a last faint attempt at joviality, 'It's all over now, you know: how's grandfather? Very much frightened still – eh?'

'Oh, sir! frightened, I'm afraid out of his mind!' and unable to control herself any longer, poor Annie fairly burst into tears.

'Don't cry, Annie! no crying! I can't stand it – you musn't really!' said the Squire in anything but steady tones, 'I'll talk him back into his mind; I will, as sure as my name's Matthew Colebatch: – Stop!' (here he pulled out his voluminous India pocket-handkerchief, and began very gently and caressingly to wipe away her tears, as if she had been a little child, and his own daughter). 'There, now we've dried them up – no we hav'nt! there's one left – And now that's gone, let's have a little talk about this business, my dear, and see what's to be done. In the first place, what's all this I hear about a plaster cast being broken?'

Annie would have given the world to open her heart about the mask of Shakspeare, to Mr Colebatch; but she thought of her promise, and she thought, also, of the Town Council of Stratford, who might hear of the secret somehow, if it was once disclosed to anybody; and might pursue her grandfather with all the powers of the law, miserable and shattered though he now was, even to his hiding-place, at Tidbury-on-the-Marsh.

'I've promised, sir, not to say anything about the plaster-cast to anybody,' she began, looking very embarrassed and unhappy.

'And you'll keep your promise,' interposed the Squire; 'that's right – good, honest little girl! I like you all the better for it; we won't say a word more about the cast; but what have they taken? what have the infernal scoundrels taken?'

'Grandfather's old silver watch, sir, and his purse with seventeen and sixpence in it, and my brooch – but that's nothing.'

'Nothing! Annie's brooch nothing!' cried the Squire, recovering his constitutional testiness: 'But, never mind, I'm determined to have the rascals caught and hung, if it's only for stealing that brooch! And now, look here, my dear; if you don't want to put me into one of my passions, take that, and say nothing about it!'

'Take' what? gracious powers! 'take' Golconda! he had crumpled a ten pound note into her hand!

'I say, again, you obstinate little thing, don't put me in one of my passions!' exclaimed the old gentleman, as poor Annie made some faint show of difficulty in taking the gift. 'God forbid I should think of hurting your feelings, my dear, for such a paltry reason as having a few more pounds in *my* pocket, than you have in *yours!*' he continued, in such serious, kind tones, that Annie's eyes began to fill again. 'We'll call that banknote, if you like, payment beforehand, for a large order for lace, from me. I saw you making lace, you know, yesterday; and I mean to consider you my lace-manufacturer in ordinary, for the rest of your life. By George!' – he went on, resuming his odd abrupt manner, -- 'it's unknown the quantity of lace I shall want to buy! There's my old housekeeper, Mrs Buddle – hang me, Annie, if I don't dress her in nothing but lace, from top to toe, inside and out, all over! Only mind this, you don't set to work at the order till I tell you! We must wait till Mrs Buddle has worn out her old stock of petticoats, before we begin – eh? There! there! there! don't go crying again! Can I see Mr Wray? No? – Quite right! better not disturb him so soon. Give him my compliments, and say I'll call to-morrow. Put up the note! put up the note! and don't be low-spirited – and don't do another thing, little Annie; don't forget you've got a queer old friend, who lives at Cropley Court!'

Running on in this way, the good Squire fairly talked himself out of the room, without letting Annie get in a word edgewise. Once on the stairs, he fell foul of the house-breakers again, with undiminished fury. The last thing the landlady heard him say, as she closed the street-door after him, was, that he was off now, to 'trounce' the two Tidbury watchmen, for not stopping the robbery – to 'trounce them handsomely,' as sure as his name was Matthew Colebatch!

Carefully putting away the kind old gentleman's gift, (they were penniless before she received it), Annie returned to her grandfather's room. He had altered a little, as the morning advanced, and was now occupied over an employment which it wrung her heart to see, – he was trying to restore the mask of Shakspeare.

The first words he had spoken since the burglary, were addressed to Annie. He seemed not to know that the robbers had effected their retreat, before she got down stairs; and asked whether they had hurt her. Calmed on this point, he next beckoned the carpenter to him, and entreated, in an eager whisper, to have some glue made directly. They could not imagine, at first, what he wanted it for; but they humoured him gladly.

When the glue was brought, he opened his cash-box, with a look of faint pining hope in his face, that it was very mournful to see, and began to arrange the fragments of the mask, on the bed before him. They were shattered past all mending; but still he moved them about here and there, with his trembling hands, murmuring sadly, all the while, that he knew it was very difficult, but felt sure he should succeed at last. Sometimes he selected the pieces wrongly; stuck, perhaps, two or three together with the glue; and then had to pull them apart again. Even when he chose the fragments properly, he could not find enough that would join sufficiently well to re-produce only one poor quarter of the mask in its former shape. Still he went on, turning over piece after piece of the broken plaster, down to the very smallest, patiently and laboriously, with the same false hope of success, and the same vain perseverance under the most disheartening failure, animating him for hours together. He had begun early in the morning – he had not given up, when Annie returned from her interview with Mr Colebatch. To know how utterly fruitless all his efforts must be, and still to see him so anxiously continuing them in spite of failure, was a sight to despair over, and to tremble at, indeed.

At last, Annie entreated him to put the fragments away in the box, and take a little rest. He would listen to nobody else; but he listened to her, and did what she asked; saying that his head was not clear enough for the work of repairing, to-day; but that he felt certain he should succeed to-morrow. When he had locked the box, and put it under his pillow, he laid back, and fell into a sleep directly.

Such was his condition! Every idea was now out of his mind, but the idea of restoring the mask of Shakspeare. Divert him from that; and he either fell asleep, or sat up vacant and speechless. It was suspension, not loss of the faculties, with *him*. The fibre of his mind relaxed with the breaking of the beloved possession to which it had been attached. Those still, cold, plaster features had been his thought by day, his dream by night; in them, his deep and beautiful devotion to Shakspeare – beautiful as an innate poetic faith that had lived through every poetic privation of life – had found its dearest outward manifestation. All about that mask, he had unconsciously hung fresh votive offerings of pride and pleasure, and humble happiness, almost with every fresh hour. It had been the one great achievement of his life, to get it; and the one great determination of his life, to keep it. And now it was broken! The dearest household-god, next to his grandchild, that the poor actor had ever had to worship, his own eyes had seen lying shattered on the floor!

It was this – far more than the fright produced by the burglary, – that had altered him, as he was altered now.

There was no rousing him. Every-body tried, and everybody failed. He went on patiently, day after day, at his miserably hopeless task of joining the fragments of the plaster; and always had some excuse for failure, always some reason for beginning the attempt anew. Annie could influence him in everything else, – for his heart, which was all hers, had escaped the blow that had stunned his mind, – but, on any subject connected with the mask, her interference was powerless.

The good squire came to try what he could do – came every day; and joked, entreated, lectured, and advised, in his own hearty, eccentric manner; but the old man only smiled faintly; and forgot what had been said to him, as soon as the words were out of the sayer's mouth. Mr Colebatch, reduced to his last resources, hit on what he considered a first-rate stratagem. He privately informed Annie, that he would insist on his whole establishment of servants, with Mrs Buddle, the housekeeper, at their head, learning elocution; so as to employ Mr Wray again, in a duty he was used to perform. 'None of those infernal Tidbury people will learn,' said the kind old squire; 'so my servants shall make a class for him, with Mrs Buddle at the top, to keep them in order. Set him teaching in his own way; and he must come round – he *must* from force of habit!' But he did not. They told him a class of new pupils was waiting for him; he just answered he was very glad to hear it; and forgot all about the matter the moment afterwards.

The doctor endeavoured to help them. He tried stimulants, and tried sedatives; he tried keeping his patient in bed, and tried keeping him up; he tried blistering, and tried cupping; and then he gave over; saying that Mr Wray must certainly have something on his mind, and that physic and regimen were of no use. One word of comfort, however, the doctor still had to speak. The physical strength of the old man had failed him very little, as yet. He was always ready to be got out of bed, and dressed; and seemed glad when he was seated in his chair. This was a good sign; but there was no telling how long it might last.

It had lasted a whole week – a long, blank, melancholy winter's week! And now, Christmas Day was fast coming: coming for the first time as a day of mourning, to the little family who, in spite of poverty and all poverty's hardening disasters, had hitherto enjoyed it happily and lovingly together, as the blessed holiday of the whole year! Ah! how doubly heavy-hearted poor Annie felt, as she entered her bedroom for the night, and remembered that that day fortnight would be Christmas Day!

She was beginning to look wan and thin already. It is not joy only, that shows soonest and plainest in the young; grief – alas that it should be so! – shares, in this world, the same privilege: and Annie now looked, as she felt, sick at heart. That day had brought no change: she had left the old man for the night, and left him no better. He had passed hours again, in trying to restore the mask; still instinctively exhibiting from time to time some fondness and attention towards his grandchild – but just as hopelessly vacant to every other influence as ever.

Annie listlessly sat down on the one chair in her small bed-room, thinking (it was her only thought now,) of what new plan could be adopted to rouse her grandfather on the morrow; and still mourning over the broken mask, as the one fatal obstacle to every effort she could try. Thus she sat for some minutes, languid and dreamy – when, suddenly, a startling and a wonderful change came over her, worked from within. She bounded up from her chair, as dead-pale and as dead-still as if she had been struck to stone. Then, a moment after, her face flushed crimson, she clasped her hands violently together, and drew her breath quick. And then, the paleness came once more – she trembled all over – and knelt down by the bedside, hiding her face in her hands.

When she rose again, the tears were rolling fast over her cheeks. She poured out some water, and washed them away. A strange expression of firmness – a glow of enthusiasm, beautiful in its brightness and purity – overspread her face, as she took up her candle, and left the room.

She went to the very top of the house, where the carpenter slept; and knocked at his door.

'Are you not gone to bed yet, Martin?' – she whispered – (the old joke of calling him 'Julius Caesar' was all over now!)

He opened the door in astonishment, saying he had only that moment got up stairs.

'Come down to the drawing-room, Martin,' she said; looking brightly on him – almost wildly, as *he* thought. 'Come quick! I must speak to you at once.'

He followed her down stairs. When they got into the drawing-room, she carefully closed the door; and then said:–

'A thought has come to me, Martin, that I *must* tell you. It came to me just now, when I was alone in my room; and I believe God sent it!'

She beckoned to him to sit by her side; and then began to whisper in his ear – quickly, eagerly, without pause.

His face began to turn pale at first, as hers had done, while he listened. Then it flushed, then grew firm like hers, but in a far stronger degree. When she had finished speaking, he only said, it was a terrible risk every way – repeating '*every way*,' with strong emphasis; but that she wished it; and therefore it should be done.

As they rose to separate, she said tenderly and gravely:–

'You have always been very good to me, Martin: be good, and be a brother to me more than ever now – for now I am trusting you with all I have to trust.'

Years afterwards when they were married, and when their children were growing up around them, he remembered Annie's last look, and Annie's last words, as they parted that night.

CHAPTER IX

THE MASK OF SHAKSPEARE

The next morning, when the old man was ready to get out of bed and be dressed, it was not the honest carpenter who came to help him as usual, but a stranger – the landlady's brother. He never noticed this change. What thoughts he had left, were all pre-occupied. The evening before, from an affectionate wish to humour him in the caprice which had become the one leading idea of his life, Annie had bought for him a bottle of cement. And now, he went on murmuring to himself, all the while he was being dressed, about the certainty of his succeeding at last in piecing together the broken fragments of the mask, with the aid of this cement. It was only the glue, he said, that had made him fail hitherto; with cement to aid him, he was quite certain of success.

The landlady and her brother helped him down into the drawing-room. Nobody was there; but on the table, where the breakfast-things were laid, was placed a small note. He looked round inquisitively when he first saw that the apartment was empty. Then, the only voice within him that was not silenced – the voice of his heart – spoke, and told him that Annie ought to have been in the room to meet him as usual.

'Where is she?' he asked eagerly.

'Don't leave me alone with him, James,' whispered the landlady to her brother, 'there's bad news to tell him.'

'Where is she?' he reiterated; and his eye got a wild look, as he asked the question for the second time.

'Pray, compose yourself, sir; and read that letter,' said the landlady, in soothing tones; 'Miss Annie's quite safe, and wants you to read this.' She handed him the letter.

He struck it away; so fiercely that she started back in terror. Then he cried out violently for the third time:

'Where is she?'

'Tell him,' whispered the landlady's brother, 'tell him at once, or you'll make him worse.'

'Gone, sir,' said the woman – 'gone away; but only for three days. The last words she said were, tell my grandfather I shall be back in three days; and give him that letter with my dearest love. Oh, don't look so, sir – don't look so! She's sure to be back.'

He was muttering 'gone' several times to himself, with a fearful expression of vacancy in his eyes. Suddenly, he signed to have the letter picked up from the ground; tore it open the moment it was given to him; and began to try to read the contents.

The letter was short, and written in very blotted unsteady characters. It ran thus:–

'Dearest Grandfather, – I never left you before in my life; and I only go now to try and serve you, and do you good. In three days, or sooner, if God pleases, I will come back, bringing something with me that will gladden your heart, and make you love me even better than ever. I dare not tell you where I am going, or what I am going for – you would be so frightened, and would perhaps send after me to fetch me back; but believe there is no danger! And, oh, dear dear grandfather, don't doubt your little Annie; and don't doubt I will be back as I say, bringing something to make you forgive me for going away without your leave. We shall be so happy again, if you will only wait the three days! *He* – you know who – goes with me, to take care of me. Think, dear grandfather, of the blessed Christmas time that will bring us all together again, happier than ever! I can't write any more, but that I pray God to bless and keep you, till we meet again! – ANNIE WRAY.'

He had not read the letter more than half through, when he dropped it, uttering the one word, 'gone,' in a shrill scream, that it made them shudder to hear. Then, it seemed as if a shadow, an awful, indescribable shadow, were stealing over his face. His fingers worked and fidgetted with an end of the tablecloth close by him; and he began to speak in faint whispering tones.

'I'm afraid I'm going mad; I'm afraid something's frightened me out of my wits,' he murmured, under his breath. 'Stop! let me try if I know anything. There now! there! That's the breakfast-table: I know that. There's *her* cup and saucer; and there's mine. Yes! and that third-place, on the other side, whose is that? – whose, whose, whose? Ah! my God! my God! I *am* mad! I've forgotten that third place!' He stopped, shivering all over. Then, the moment after, he shrieked out – 'Gone! who says she's gone? It's a lie; no, no, it's a cruel joke put upon me. Annie! I won't be joked with. Come down, Annie! Call her, some of you! Annie! they've broken it all to pieces – the plaster won't stick together again! You can't leave me, now they've broken it all to pieces! Annie! Annie! come and mend it! Annie! little Annie!'

He called on her name for the last time, in tones of entreaty unutterably plaintive; then sank down on a chair, moaning; then became silent – doggedly silent – and fiercely suspicious of everything. In that mood he remained, till his strength began to fail him; and then he let them lead him to the sofa. When he lay down, he fell off quickly into a heavy, feverish slumber.

Ah, Annie! Annie! carefully as you watched him, you knew but little of his illness; you never foreboded such a result of your absence as this; or, brave and loving as your purpose was in leaving him, you would have shrunk from the fatal necessity of quitting his bed-side for three days together!

Mr Colebatch came in shortly after the old man had fallen asleep, accompanied by a new doctor – a medical man of great renown, who had stolen a little time from his London practice, partly to visit some relations who lived at Tidbury, and partly to recruit his own health, which had suffered in repairing other people's. The good Squire, the moment he heard that such assistance as this was accidentally available in the town, secured it for poor old Reuben, without a moment's delay.

'Oh, sir!' said the landlady, meeting them down stairs; 'he's been going on in such a dreadful way! What are we to do, I really don't know.'

'It's lucky somebody else does,' interrupted the Squire, peevishly.

'But you don't know, sir, that Miss Annie's gone – gone without saying where!'

'Yes, I happen to know that too!' said Mr Colebatch; 'I've got a letter from her, asking me to take care of her grandfather, while she's away; and here I am to do what she tells me. First of all, ma'am, let us get into some room, where this gentleman and I can have five minutes' talk in private.'

'Now, sir' – said the Squire, when he and the doctor were closeted together in the back parlour – 'the long and the short of the case is this: – A week ago, two infernal housebreakers broke into this house, and found old Mr Wray sitting up alone in the drawing-room. Of course, they frightened him out of his wits; and they stole some trifles too – but that's nothing. They managed somehow to break a plaster cast of his. There's a mystery about this cast, that the family won't explain, and that nobody can find out; but the fact appears to be, that the old man was as fond of his cast as if it was one of his children – a queer thing, you'll say; but true, sir; true as my name's Colebatch! Well: ever since, he's been weak in his mind; always striving to mend this wretched cast, and taking no notice of anything else. This sort of thing has lasted for six or seven days. – And now, another mystery! I get a letter from his grand-daughter – the kindest, dearest little thing! – begging me to look after him – you never saw such a lovely, tender-hearted letter! – to look after him, I say, while she's gone for three days, to come back with a surprise for him that she says will work miracles. She don't say what surprise – or, where she's going – but she promises to come back in three days; and she'll do it! I'll stake my existence on little Annie sticking to her word! Now the question is – till we see her again, and all this precious mystery's cleared up – what are we to do for the poor old man? – what? – eh?'

'Perhaps' – said the doctor, smiling at the conclusion of this characteristic harangue – 'perhaps, I had better see the patient, before we say any more.'

'By George! what a fool I am!' – cried the Squire – 'Of course! – see him directly – this way, doctor; this way!'

They went into the drawing-room. The sufferer was still on the sofa, moving and talking in his sleep. The doctor signed to Mr Colebatch to keep silence; and they sat down and listened.

The old man's dreams seemed to be connected with some of the later scenes in his life, which had been passed at country towns, in teaching country actors. He was laughing just at this moment.

'Ho! Ho! young gentlemen' – they heard him say – 'do you call that acting? Ah, dear! dear! we professional people don't bump against each other on the stage, in that way – it's lucky you called me in, before your friends came to see you! – Stop, sir! that won't do! you mustn't die in that way – fall on your knee first; then sink down – then – Oh, dear! how hard it is to get people to have a proper delivery, and not go dropping their voices, at the end of every sentence. I shall never – never——'

Here the wild words stopped; then altered, and grew sad.

'Hush! Hush!' – he murmured, in husky, wandering tones – 'Silence there, behind the scenes! Don't you hear Mr Kemble speaking now? listen, and get a lesson, as I do. Ah! laugh away, fools, who don't know good acting when you see it! – Let me alone! What are you pushing me for? I'm doing *you* no harm! I'm only looking at Mr Kemble – Don't touch that book! – it's *my* Shakspeare – yes! mine. I suppose I may read Shakspeare if I like, though I *am* only an actor at a shilling a night! – A shilling a night; – starving wages – Ha! Ha! Ha! – starving wages!'

Again the sad strain altered to a still wilder and more plaintive key.

'Ah!' he cried now, 'don't be hard with me! Don't, for God's sake! My wife, my poor dear wife, died only a week ago! Oh, I'm cold! starved with cold here, in this draughty place. I can't help crying, sir; she was so good to me! But I'll take care and go on the stage when I'm called to go, if you'll please not take any notice of me now; and not let them laugh at me. Oh, Mary! Mary! Why has God taken you from me? Ah! why! why! why!'

Here, the murmurs died away; then began again, but more confusedly. Sometimes his wandering speech was all about Annie; sometimes it changed to lamentations over the broken mask; sometimes it went back again to the old days behind the scenes at Drury Lane.

'Oh, Annie! Annie!' cried the Squire, with his eyes full of tears; 'why did you ever go away?'

'I am not sure,' said the doctor, 'that her going may not do good in the end. It has evidently brought matters to a climax with him; I can see that. Her coming back will be a shock to his mind – it's a risk, sir; but that shock may act in the right way. When a man's faculties struggle to recover themselves, as his are doing, those faculties are not altogether gone. The young lady will come back, you say, the day after to-morrow?'

'Yes, yes!' answered the Squire, 'with a "surprise," she says. What surprise? Good Heavens! why couldn't she say what!'

'We need not mind that,' rejoined the other. '*Any* surprise will do, if his physical strength will bear it. We'll keep him quiet – as much asleep as possible – till she comes back. I've seen some very curious cases of this kind, Mr Colebatch; cases that were cured by the merest accidents, in the most unaccountable manner. I shall watch this particular case with interest.'

'Cure it, doctor! cure it; and, by Jupiter! I'll——'

'Hush! you'll wake him. We had better go now. I shall come back in an hour, and will tell the landlady where she can let me know, if anything happens before that.'

They went out softly; and left him as they had found him, muttering and murmuring in his sleep.

★ ★ ★

On the third day, late in the afternoon, Mr Colebatch and the doctor were again in the drawing-room at No. 12; and again intently occupied in studying the condition of poor old Reuben Wray.

This time, he was wide-awake; and was restlessly and feebly moving up and down the room, talking to himself, now mournfully about the broken mask, now fiercely and angrily about Annie's absence. Nothing attracted his notice in the smallest degree; he seemed to be perfectly unaware that anybody was in the room with him.

'Why can't you keep him quiet,' whispered the Squire; 'why don't you give him an opiate, or whatever you call it, as you did yesterday?'

'His grandchild comes back to-day,' answered the doctor. 'To-day must be left to the great physician – Nature. At this crisis, it is not for me to meddle, but to watch and learn.'

They waited again in silence. Lights were brought in; for it grew dark while they kept their anxious watch. Still no arrival!

Five o'clock struck; and, about ten minutes after, a knock sounded at the street-door.

'She has come back!' exclaimed the doctor.

'How do you know that already?' asked Mr Colebatch, eagerly.

'Look there, sir!' and the doctor pointed to Mr Wray.

He had been moving about with increased restlessness, and talking with increased vehemence, just before the knock. The moment it sounded, he stopped; and there he stood now, perfectly speechless and perfectly still. There was no expression on his face. His very breathing seemed suspended. What secret influences were moving within him now? What dread command went forth over the dark waters in which his spirit toiled, saying to them, 'Peace! be still!' That, no man – not even the man of science – could tell.

As the door opened, and the landlady's joyful exclamation of recognition, sounded cheerily from below, the doctor rose from his seat, and gently placed himself close behind the old man.

Footsteps hurried up the stairs. Then, Annie's voice was heard, breathless and eager, before she came in. 'Grandfather, I've got the mould! Grandfather, I've brought a new cast! The mask – thank God! – the mask of Shakspeare!'

She flew into his arms, without even a look at anybody else in the room. When her head was on his bosom, the spirit of the brave little girl deserted her for the first time since her absence, and she burst into an hysterical passion of weeping before she could utter another word.

He gave a great cry the moment she touched him – an inarticulate voice of recognition from the spirit within. Then his arms closed tight over her; so tight, that the doctor advanced a step or two towards them, showing in his face the first look of alarm it had yet betrayed.

But, at that instant, the old man's arms dropped again, powerless and heavy, by his side. What does he see now, in that open box in the carpenter's hand? The Mask! – *his* Mask, whole as ever! white, and smooth, and beautiful, as when he first drew it from the mould, in his own bedroom at Stratford!

The struggle of the vital principle at that sight – the straining and writhing of every nerve – was awful to look on. His eyes rolled, distended, in their orbits; a dark red flush of blood heaved up and overspread his face; he drew his breath in heavy, hoarse gasps of agony. This lasted for a moment – one dread moment; then he fell forward, to all appearance death-struck, in the doctor's arms.

He was borne to the sofa, amid the silence of that suspense which is too terrible for words. The doctor laid his finger on his wrist, waited an instant, then looked up, and slightly nodded his head. The pulse was feebly beating again, already!

Long and delicate was the process of restoring him to animation. It was like aiding the faint new life to develope itself in a child just born. But the doctor was as patient as he was skilful; and they heard the old man draw his breath again, gently and naturally, at last.

His weakness was so great, that his eyelids closed at his first effort to look round him. When they opened again, his eyes seemed strangely liquid and soft – almost like the eyes of a young girl. Perhaps this was partly because they turned on Annie the moment they could see.

Soon, his lips moved; but his voice was so faint, that the doctor was obliged to listen close at his mouth to hear him. He said, in fluttering accents, that he had had a *dreadful dream*, which had made him very ill, he was afraid; but that it was all over, and he was better now, though not quite strong enough to receive so many visitors yet. Here his strength for speaking failed, and he looked round on Annie again in silence. In a minute more he whispered to her. She went to the table and fetched the new mask; and, kneeling down, held it before him to look at.

The doctor beckoned Mr Colebatch, the landlady, and the carpenter, to follow him into the back-room.

'Now,' said he, 'I've one, and only one, important direction to give you all; and you must communicate it to Miss Wray when she is a little less agitated. On no account let the patient imagine he's wrong in thinking that all his troubles have been the troubles of a dream. That will be the weak point in his intellectual consciousness for the rest of his life. When he gets stronger, he is sure to question you curiously about this dream; keep him in his self-deceit, as you value his sanity! He's only got his reason back by getting it out of the very jaws of death, I can tell you – give it full time to strengthen! You know, I dare say, that a joint which is dislocated by a jerk, is also replaced by a jerk. Consider his mind, in the same way, to have been dislocated by one shock, and now replaced by another; and treat his intellect as you would treat a limb that had only just been slipped back into its proper place – treat it tenderly. By the bye,' added the doctor, after a moment's consideration, 'if you can't get the key of his box, without suspicion, pick the lock; and throw away the fragments of the old cast (which he was always talking about in his delirium) – destroy them altogether. If he ever sees them again, they may do him dreadful mischief. He must always imagine what he imagines at present, that the new cast is the same cast that he has had all along. It's a very remarkable case, Mr Colebatch, very remarkable: I really feel indebted to you for enabling me to study it. Compose yourself, sir, you're a little shaken and startled by this, I see; but there's no danger for him now. Look there: that man, except on one point, is as sane as ever he was in his life!'

They looked, as the doctor spoke. Mr Wray was still on the sofa, gazing at the mask of Shakspeare, which Annie supported before him, as she knelt by his side. His arm was round her neck; and, from time to time, he whispered to her, smiling faintly, but very happily, as she replied in whispers also. The sight was simple enough; but the landlady, thinking on all that had passed, began to weep as she beheld it. The honest carpenter looked very ready to follow her example; and Mr Colebatch probably shared the same weakness at that moment, though he was less candid in betraying it. 'Come,' said the Squire, very huskily and hastily, 'we are only in the way here; let us leave them together!'

'Quite right, sir,' observed the doctor; 'that pretty little girl is the only medical attendant fit to be with him now! I wait for *you* Mr Colebatch!'

'I say, young fellow,' said the Squire to the carpenter, as they went down stairs, 'be in the way to-morrow morning: I've a good deal to ask you in private when I'm not all over in a twitter, as I am at present. Now our good old friend's getting round, my curiosity's getting round too. Be in the way to-morrow, at ten, when I come here. Quite ready, doctor! No! after *you*, if you please. Ah, thank God! we came into this house mourners, and we go out of it to rejoice. It will be a happy Christmas, doctor, and a merry New Year, after all!'

CHAPTER X

CHRISTMAS TIME

When ten o'clock came, the Squire came – punctual to a minute. Instead of going up stairs, he mysteriously sent for the carpenter into the back parlour.

'Now, in the first place, how is Mr Wray?' – said the old gentleman, as anxiously as if he had not already sent three times the night before, and twice earlier in the morning, to ask that very question.

'Lord bless you, sir!' – answered the carpenter with a grin, and a very expressive rubbing of the hands – 'He's coming to again, after his nice sleep last night, as brave as ever. He's dreadful weak still, to be sure; but he's got like himself again, already. He's been down on me twice in the last half hour, sir, about my elocution; he's making Annie read Shakspeare to him; and he's asking whether any new pupils are coming – all just in the old way again. Oh, sir, it is so jolly to see him like that once more – if you'll only come up stairs——'

'Stop, till we've had our talk' – said the Squire – 'sit down. By the bye! has he said anything yet about that infernal cash-box?'

'I picked the lock of the box this morning, sir, as the gentleman told me; and buried every bit of plaster out of it, deep in the kitchen garden. He saw the box afterwards, and gave a tremble, like. "Take it away," says he, "never let me see it again: it reminds me of that dreadful dream." And then, sir, he told us about what happened, just as if he really *had* dreamt it; saying he couldn't get the subject quite out of his head, the whole thing was so much as if it had truly taken place. Afterwards, sir, he thanked me for making the new box for the cast – he remembered my promising to do that, though it was only just before all our trouble!'

'And of course, you humour him in everything, and let him think he's right?' – said the Squire – 'He must never know that he hasn't been dreaming, to his dying day.'

And he never did know it – never, in *this* world, had even a suspicion of what he owed to Annie! It was but little matter; they could not have loved each other better, if he had discovered everything.

'Now, master carpenter,' pursued the Squire, 'you've answered very nicely hitherto. Just answer as nicely the next question I ask. What's the whole history of this mysterious plaster cast? It's no use fidgetting! I've seen the cast; I know it's a portrait of Shakspeare! and I've made up my mind to find out all about it. Do you mean to say you think I'm not a friend fit to be trusted? Eh, you sir?'

'I never could think so, after all your goodness, sir. But, if you please, I really did promise to keep the thing a secret,' said the carpenter, looking very much as if he were watching his opportunity to open the door, and run out of the room; 'I promised, sir; I did, indeed!'

'Promised a fiddlestick!' exclaimed the Squire, in a passion. 'What's the use of keeping a secret that's half let out already? I'll tell you what, you Mr ——, what's your name? There's some joke about calling you Julius Caesar. What's your real name, if you really have one?'

'Martin Blunt, sir. But don't, pray don't ask me to tell the secret! I don't say *you* would blab it, sir; but if it *did* leak out, like; and get to Stratford-upon-Avon,' – here he suddenly became silent, feeling he was beginning to commit himself already.

'Stop! I've got it!' cried Mr Colebatch. 'Hang me, if I haven't got it at last!'

'Don't tell *me*, sir! Pray don't tell me, if you have!'

'Stick to your chair, Mr Martin Blunt! No shirking with *me*! I was a fool not to suspect the thing, the moment I saw it was a portrait of Shakspeare. I've seen the Stratford bust, Master Blunt! You're afraid of Stratford, are you? – Why? I know! Some of you have been taking that cast from the Stratford bust, without leave – it's as like it, as two peas! Now, young fellow, I'll tell you what! if you don't make a clean breast to me at once, I'm off to the office of the "Tidbury Mercury," to put in my version of the whole thing, as a good local anecdote! Will you tell me? or will you not? – I'm asking this in Mr Wray's interests, or I'd die before I asked you at all!'

Confused, threatened, bullied, bawled at, and out-manoeuvred, the unfortunate carpenter fairly gave way. 'If it's wrong in me to tell you, sir, it's your fault what I do,' said the simple fellow; and he forthwith retailed, in a very roundabout, stammering manner, the whole of the disclosure he had heard from old Reuben – the Squire occasionally throwing in an explosive interjection of astonishment, or admiration; but, otherwise, receiving the narrative with remarkable calmness and attention.

'What the deuce is all this nonsense about the Stratford town-council, and the penalties of the law?' – cried Mr Colebatch, when the carpenter had done – 'But never mind; we can come to that afterwards. Now tell me about going back to get the mould out of the cupboard, and making the new cast. I know who did it! It's that dear, darling, incomparable little girl! – but tell me all about it – come! quick, quick! – don't keep me waiting!'

'Julius Caesar' got on with his second narrative much more glibly than with the first. How Annie had suddenly remembered, one night, in her bed-room, about the mould having been left behind – how she was determined to try and restore her grandfather's health and faculties, by going to seek it; and how he (the carpenter), had gone also, to protect her – how they got to Stratford, by the coach (outside places, in the cold, to save money) – how Annie appealed to the mercy of their former landlord; and instead of inventing some falsehood to deceive him, fairly told her whole story in all its truth – how the landlord pitied them, and promised to keep their secret – how they went up into the bed-room, and found the mould in the old canvas bag, behind the volumes of the 'Annual Register,' just where Mr Wray had left it – how Annie, remembering what her grandfather had told her, about the process of making a cast, bought plaster, and followed out her instructions; failing in the first attempt, but admirably succeeding in the second – how they were obliged, in frightful suspense, to wait till the third day for the return-coach; and how they finally got back, safe and sound, not only with the new cast, but with the mould as well. – All these particulars flowed from the carpenter's lips, in a strain of homely eloquence, which no elocutionary aid could have furnished with one atom of additional effect, that would have done it any good whatever.

'We'd no notion, sir,' said 'Julius Caesar,' in conclusion, 'that poor Mr Wray was so bad as he really was, when we went away. It was a dreadful trial to Annie, sir, to go. She went down on her knees to the landlady – I saw her do it, half wild, like; she was in such a state – she went down on her knees, sir, to ask the woman to be as a daughter to the old man, till she came back. Well, sir, even after that, it was a toss-up whether she went away, when the morning came. But she was obliged to do it. She durstn't trust me to go alone, for fear I should let the mould tumble down, when I got it (which I'm afraid, sir, was very likely!) – or get into some scrape, by telling *what* I oughtn't, *where* I oughtn't; and so be taken up, mould and all, before the Town Council, who were going to put Mr Wray in prison, only we ran off to Tidbury; and so——'

'Nonsense! stuff! they could no more put him in prison for taking the cast than I can,' cried the Squire. 'Stop! I've got a thought! I've got a thought at least, that's worth – Is the mould here? – Yes or No?'

'Yes, sir! Bless us and save us, what's the matter!'

'Run!' cried Mr Colebatch, pacing up and down the room like mad. 'No. 15 in the street! Dabbs and Clutton, the lawyers! Fetch one of them in a second! Damn it, run! or I shall burst a blood-vessel!'

The carpenter ran *to* No. 15; and Mr Dabbs, who happened to be in, ran *from* No. 15. Mr Colebatch met him at the street-door, dragged him into the back parlour, pushed him on to a chair, and instantly stated the case between Mr Wray and the authorities at Stratford, in the fewest possible words and the hastiest possible tones.

'Now,' said the old gentleman at the end, 'can they, or can they not, hurt him for what he's done?'

'It's a very nice point,' said Mr Dabbs, 'a very nice point indeed, sir.'

'Hang it, man!' cried the Squire, 'don't talk to *me* about "nice points," as if a point was something good to eat! Can they, or can they not, hurt him? Answer that in three words!'

'They can't,' said Dabbs, answering it triumphantly in two.

'Why?' asked the Squire, beating him by a rejoinder in one.

'For this reason,' said Dabbs. 'What does Mr Wray take with him into the church? Plaster of his own, in powder. What does he bring out with him? The same plaster, in another form. Does any right of copyright reside in a bust two hundred years old? Impossible. Has Mr Wray hurt the bust? No; or they would have found him out here, and prosecuted directly – for they know where he is. I heard of the thing from a Stratford man, yesterday, who said they knew he was at Tidbury. Under all these circumstances, where's there a shadow of a case against Mr Wray? Nowhere!'

'Capital, Dabbs! capital! you'll be Lord Chancellor some day: never heard a better opinion in my life! Now, Mr Julius Caesar Blunt, do you see what my thought is? No! Look here. Take casts from that mould till your arms ache again; clap them upon slabs of black marble to show off the white face; sell them, at a guinea each, to the loads of people who would give anything to have a portrait of Shakspeare; and then open your breeches' pockets fast enough to let the gold tumble in, if you can! Tell Mr Wray that; and you tell him he's a rich man, or – no don't, you're no more fit to do it properly than I am! Tell every syllable you've heard here to Annie, directly; she'll know how to break it to him; go! be off!'

'But what are we to say about how we got the mould here, sir? We can't tell Mr Wray the truth.'

'Tell him a flam, of course! Say it's been found in the cupboard, by the landlord, at Stratford, and sent on here. Dabbs will bear witness that the Stratford people know he's at Tidbury, and know they can't touch him: he's sure to think *that* a pretty good proof that we are right. Say I bullied you out of the secret, when I saw the mould come here – say anything – but only go, and settle matters at once! I'm off to take my walk, and see about the black slabs at the stone-mason's. I'll be back in an hour, and see Mr Wray.'

The next moment, the impetuous old Squire was out of the house; and before the hour was up, he was in it again, rather more impetuous than ever.

When he entered the drawing-room, the first sight that greeted him was the carpenter, hanging up a box containing the mask (with the lid taken off) boldly and publicly over the fire-place.

'I'm glad to see that, sir,' said Mr Colebatch, shaking hands with Mr Wray. 'Annie has told you my good news, – eh?'

'Yes, sir,' answered the old man; 'the best news I've heard for some time: I can hang up my treasure there, now, where I can see it all day. It was rather too bad, sir, of those Stratford people to go frightening me, by threatening what they couldn't do. The best man among them is the man who was my landlord; he's an honest, careful fellow, to send me back my old canvas bag, and the mould (which must have seemed worthless to him), just because they were belonging to me, and left in my bedroom.

I'm rather proud, sir, of making that mask. I can never repay you for your kindness in defending my character, and taking me up as you've done – but if you would accept a copy of the cast, now we have the mould to take it from, as Annie says——'

'That I will, and thankfully,' said the Squire, 'and I order five more copies, as presents to my friends, when you begin to sell to the public.'

'I really don't know, sir, about that,' said Mr Wray, rather uneasily. 'Selling the cast is like making my great treasure very common; it's like giving up my particular possession to everybody.'

Mr Colebatch parried this objection instantly. Could Mr Wray, he asked, seriously mean to be so selfish as to deny to the other lovers of Shakspeare the privilege he prized to much himself, of possessing Shakspeare's portrait? – to say nothing of as good as plumply refusing a pretty round sum of money at the same time. Could he be selfish enough, and inconsiderate enough to do that? No: Mr Wray, on consideration, allowed he could not. He saw the subject in a new light now; and, begging Mr Colebatch's pardon, if he had seemed selfish or unthankful, he would take the Squire's advice.

'That's right!' said the old gentleman. 'Now I'm happy. You'll soon be strong enough, my good friend, to take the cast yourself.'

'I hope so,' said Mr Wray. 'It's very odd that a mere dream should make me feel so weak as I do – I suppose they told you, sir, what a horrible dream it was. If I didn't see the mask hanging up there now, as whole as ever, I should really believe it had been broken to pieces, just as I dreamt it. It must have been a dream, you know, sir, of course; for I dreamt that Annie had gone away and left me; and I found her at home as usual, when I woke up. It seems, too, that I'm a week or more behind-hand, in my notion about the day of the month. In short, sir, I should almost think myself bewitched,' he added, pressing his trembling hand over his forehead, 'if I didn't know it was near Christmas time, and didn't believe what sweet Will Shakspeare says in "Hamlet" – in a passage, by-the-by, sir, which Mr Kemble always regretted to see struck out of the acting copy.'

Here he began to declaim – faintly, but still with all the old Kemble cadences – the exquisite lines to which he referred; the Squire beating time to each modulation, with his forefinger:–

'Some say, that ever' gainst that season comes,
Wherein our Saviour's birth is celebrated,
This bird of dawning singeth all night long:
And then they say no spirit dares stir abroad;
The nights are wholesome; then no plantes strike,
No fairy takes, nor witch hath power to charm,
So hallow'd and so gracious is the time.'

'There's poetry!' exclaimed Mr Colebatch, looking up at the mask.
'That's a cut above my tragedy of the "Mysterious Murderess," I'm afraid.
Eh, Sir? And how you recite, – splendid! Hang it! we havn't had half our
talk, yet, about Shakspeare and John Kemble. A chat with an old stager
like you, is new life to me, in such a barbarous place as this! Ah, Mr
Wray!' (and here the Squire's voice lowered, and grew strangely tender
for such a rough old gentleman), 'you are a happy man, to have a
grandchild to keep you company at all times, but especially at Christmas
time. I'm a lonely old bachelor, and must eat my Christmas dinner
without wife or child to sweeten the taste to me of a single morsel!'

As little Annie heard this, she rose, and stole up to the Squire's side.
Her pale face was covered with blushes (all her pretty natural colour had
not come back yet); she looked softly at Mr Colebatch, for a moment –
then looked down – then said——

'Don't say you're lonely, sir! If you would let *me* be like a grandchild to
you, I should be so glad. I – I always make the plum-pudding, sir, on
Christmas Day, for grandfather – if he would allow, – and if – if you——'

'If that little love isn't trying to screw her courage up to ask me to taste
her plum-pudding, I'm a Dutchman' – cried the Squire, catching Annie
in his arms, and fairly kissing her – 'Without ceremony, Mr Wray, I
invite myself here, to a Christmas dinner. We would have had it at
Cropley Court; but you're not strong enough yet, to go out these cold
nights. Never mind! all the dinner, except Annie's pudding, shall be done
by my cook; Mrs Buddle, the housekeeper, shall come and help; and
we'll have such a feast, please God, as no king ever sat down to! No
apologies, my good friend, on either side: I'm determined to spend the
happiest Christmas Day I ever did in my life; and so shall you!'

★ ★ ★

And the good Squire kept his word. It was, of course, noised abroad over
the whole town, that Matthew Colebatch, Esquire, Lord of the Manor of
Tidbury-on-the-Marsh, was going to dine on Christmas Day with an old
player, in a lodging-house. The genteel population were universally
scandalised and indignant. The Squire had exhibited his levelling
tendencies pretty often before, they said. He had, for instance, been seen
cutting jokes in the High-street with a travelling tinker, to whom he had
applied in broad daylight to put a new ferule on his walking-stick; he had
been detected coolly eating bacon and greens in one of his tenant farmer's
cottages; he had been heard singing, 'Begone, dull care,' in a cracked tenor,
to amuse another tenant-farmer's child. These actions were disreputable
enough; but to go publicly, and dine with an obscure stage-player, put the
climax on everything! The Reverend Daubeny Daker said the Squire's

proper sphere of action, after that, was a lunatic asylum; and the Reverend Daubeny Daker's friends echoed the sentiment.

Perfectly reckless of this expression of genteel popular opinion, Mr Colebatch arrived to dinner at No. 12, on Christmas Day; and, what is more, wore his black tights and silk stockings, as if he had been going to a grand party. His dinner had arrived before him; and fat Mrs Buddle, in her lavender silk gown, with a cambric handkerchief pinned in front to keep splashes off, appeared auspiciously with the banquet. Never did Annie feel the responsibility of having a plum-pudding to make, so acutely as she felt it, on seeing the savoury feast which Mr Colebatch had ordered, to accompany her one little item of saccharine cookery.

They sat down to dinner, with the Squire at the top of the table (Mr Wray insisted on that); and Mrs Buddle at the bottom (he insisted on that also); old Reuben and Annie, at one side; and 'Julius Caesar' all by himself (they knew his habits, and gave him elbow room), at the other. Things were comparatively genteel and quiet, till Annie's pudding came in. At sight of that, Mr Colebatch set up a cheer, as if he had been behind a pack of fox-hounds. The carpenter, thrown quite off his balance by noise and excitement, knocked down a spoon, a wine-glass, and a pepper-box, one after the other, in such quick succession, that Mrs Buddle thought him mad; and Annie – for the first time, poor thing, since all her troubles – actually began to laugh again, as prettily as ever. Mr Colebatch did ample justice, it must be added, to her pudding. Twice did his plate travel up to the dish, – a third time it would have gone; but the faithful housekeeper raised her warning voice, and reminded the old gentleman that he had a stomach.

When the tables were cleared, and the glasses filled with the Squire's rare old port, that excellent man rose slowly and solemnly from his chair, announcing that he had three toasts to propose, and one speech to make; the latter, he said, being contingent on the chance of his getting properly at his voice, through two helps of plum-pudding; a chance which he thought rather remote, principally in consequence of Annie's having rather overdone the proportion of suet in mixing her ingredients.

'The first toast,' said the old gentleman, 'is the health of Mr Reuben Wray; and God bless him!' When this had been drunk with immense fervour, Mr Colebatch went on at once to his second toast, without pausing to sit down – a custom which other after-dinner orators would do well to imitate.

'The second toast,' said he, taking Mr Wray's hand, and looking at the mask, which hung opposite, prettily decorated with holly, – 'the second toast, is a wide circulation and a hearty welcome all through England, for the Mask of Shakspeare!' This was duly honoured; and immediately Mr Colebatch went on like lightning to the third toast.

'The third,' said he, 'is the speech-toast.' Here he endeavoured, unsuccessfully, to cough up his voice out of the plum-pudding. 'I say, ladies and gentlemen, this is the speech-toast.' He stopped again, and desired the carpenter to pour him out a small glass of brandy; having swallowed which, he went on fluently.

'Mr Wray, sir,' pursued the old gentleman, 'I address you in particular, because you are particularly concerned in what I am going to say. Three days ago, I had a little talk in private with those two young people. Young people, sir, are never wholly free from some imprudent tendencies; and falling in love's one of them.' (At this point, Annie slunk behind her grandfather; the carpenter, having nobody to slink behind, put himself quite at his ease, by knocking down an orange.) 'Now, sir,' continued the Squire, 'the private talk that I was speaking of, leads me to suppose that those two particular young people mean to marry each other. You, I understand, objected at first to their engagement; and like good and obedient children, they respected your objection. I think it's time to reward them for that, now. Let them marry, if they will, sir, while you can live happily to see it! I say nothing about our little darling there, but this: – the vital question for her, and for all girls, is not how *high*, but how *good*, she, and they, marry. And I must confess, I don't think she's altogether chosen so badly.' (The Squire hesitated a moment. He had in his mind, what he could not venture to speak – that the carpenter had saved old Reuben's life when the burglars were in the house; and that he had shown himself well worthy of Annie's confidence, when she asked him to accompany her, in going to recover the mould from Stratford.) 'In short sir,' Mr Colebatch resumed, – 'to cut short this speechifying, I don't think you can object to let them marry, provided they can find means of support. This, I think, they can do. First there are the profits sure to come from the mask, which you are sure to share with them, I know.' (This prophecy about the profits was fulfilled: fifty copies of the cast were ordered by the new year; and they sold better still, after that). 'This will do to begin on, I think, Mr Wray. Next, I intend to get our friend there a good berth as master-carpenter for the new Crescent they're going to build on my land, at the top of the hill – and that won't be a bad thing, I can tell you! Lastly, I mean you all to leave Tidbury, and live in a cottage of mine that's empty now, and going to rack and ruin for want of a tenant. I'll charge rent, mind, Mr Wray, and come for it every quarter myself, as regular as a tax-gatherer. I don't insult an independent man by the offer of an asylum. Heaven forbid! but till you can do better, I want you to keep my cottage warm for me. I can't give up seeing my new grandchild sometimes! and I want my chat with an old stager, about the British Drama and glorious John Kemble! To cut the thing short, sir: with such a prospect before them as this, do you object to my giving the healths of Mr and Mrs Martin Blunt that are to be!'

Conquered by the Squire's kind looks and words, as much as by his reasons, Old Reuben murmured approval of the toast, adding tenderly, as he looked round on Annie, 'If she'll only promise always to let me live with her!'

'There, there!' cried Mr Colebatch, 'don't go kissing your grandfather before company like that you little jade; making other people envious of him on Christmas Day! Listen to this! Mr and Mrs Martin Blunt that are to be – married in a week!' added the old gentleman peremptorily.

'Lord, sir!' said Mrs Buddle, 'she can't get her dresses ready in that time!'

'She *shall*, ma'am, if every mantua-making wench in Tidbury stitches her fingers off for it! and there's an end of my speech-making!' Having said this, the Squire dropped back into his chair with a gasp of satisfaction.

'Now we are all happy!' he exclaimed, filling his glass; 'and now we'll set in to enjoy our port in earnest – eh, my good friend?'

'Yes; all happy!' echoed old Reuben, patting Annie's hand, which lay in his; 'but I think I should be still happier, though, if I could only manage not to remember that horrible dream!'

'Not remember it!' cried Mr Colebatch, 'we'll all remember it – all remember it together, from this time forth, in the same pleasant way!'

'How? How?' exclaimed Mr Wray, eagerly.

'Why, my good friend!' answered the Squire, tapping him briskly on the shoulder, 'we'll all remember it gaily, as nothing but a STORY FOR A CHRISTMAS FIRESIDE!'

MISS OR MRS?

WILKIE COLLINS

Natalie Graybrooke is the only and much-loved daughter of Sir Joseph Graybrooke, a wealthy industrialist. Advised to take her on a sea voyage to restore her health, he turns to his old friend Richard Turlington, a trader of the Levant, who immediately places his schooner at Sir Joseph's disposal. Thus it is that the warm and beautiful Natalie, on the brink of womanhood, finds herself regarded by two men: Richard Turlington, to whom her dowry would be an important source of finance, and who seems to have a respectable trade and income; and Launcelot Linzie, her cousin, on board as surgeon, with whom she shares a mutual and strong attraction. As the ship makes for home, the tension between the two men heightens, and then Turlington finds that his business is facing financial collapse . . .

'Miss or Mrs?', the title story, is a typical tale of suspense by a master of the genre. The book is completed by two shorter sea stories, described by the author as being among his friend Charles Dickens's favourites.

THE NEW MAGDALEN

WILKIE COLLINS

Caught up in the midst of the war between Germany and France are two very different women: Grace Roseberry, en route to England and the care of a Lady Janet following her father's death; and Mercy Merrick who, unable to avoid the stigma of her past as a fallen woman and ex-convict, now pursues a role for herself as a nurse. As the guns fire around them, night falls. Then Grace is hit by a loose shell.

Seizing what may be her only chance to escape her past, Mercy travels to England assuming Grace's identity. But just as it seems that Mercy may at last have found both security and happiness, Lady Janet's nephew turns up, not only immediately disturbing and attracting her, but bringing with him a mysterious companion. . . .

In The New Magdalen, one of his later novels, Wilkie Collins explores contemporary attitudes to fallen women, while weaving a skilful tale from the twists of fate and fortune.

THE HAUNTED HOTEL

WILKIE COLLINS

'I want to know whether I am in danger of going mad.' When the Countess Narona meets Agnes Lockwood, the woman jilted by her husband-to-be, she feels a sense of foreboding. After the marriage, the Countess moves with her husband, Lord Montbarry, and brother, the Baron Rivar – a chemist reputed also to be a gambler – to Venice. There, disowned by his family, the Lord apparently becomes a recluse and falls fatally ill. Mystery also surrounds the unaccountable disappearance of the Lord's courier. As much as Agnes tries to forget the episode of her broken engagement, her fate and that of the Countess seem to be inextricably woven. Both are relentlessly drawn to the Palace Hotel in Venice for a final and dramatic encounter, in the room where more than past emotions resurface to haunt them. . . .

In this tale of mystery and suspense Wilkie Collins shows his masterful hand once again.

THE GUILTY RIVER

WILKIE COLLINS

Returning from years of banishment on the Continent, Gerard Roylake takes up his inheritance surrounded by strangers. His meeting with Cristel Toller, the miller's daughter, brings back happier childhood memories but also introduces him to the strangely beautiful man only known to the world as 'The Lodger'.

This sinister man, deaf and bitter in his isolation from the world, is besotted with Cristel. He exerts a peculiar influence over his surroundings and those with whom he comes into contact – but does he intend to harm Gerard Roylake, his rival for Cristel's affections? Are the fears real and the suspicions correct? Here is Wilkie Collins at his best in a superb tale reflecting the darker side of human nature.

THE WILKIE COLLINS SOCIETY

The Wilkie Collins Society was formed in 1980 to promote interest in the life and works of this important nineteenth-century author. Apart from *The Moonstone* and *The Woman in White*, which are both well known, he wrote numerous other novels, short stories, plays and essays. His books have attracted readers for more than a century and his unconventional lifestyle has intrigued the literary world for nearly as long.

The Society issues a Newsletter two or three times a year and an occasional Journal produced in the United States. There have also been reprints of Collins's short, lesser-known works. The Wilkie Collins Society has an international membership with an annual subscription of currently £7.50 (£10 overseas).

Rambles Around Marylebone, specially written for the Society by William Clark, will be sent **FREE** to new members, while supplies last.

For full details of The Wilkie Collins Society please fill in the form below:

--- ✂ ----

I would like to receive more information on The Wilkie Collins Society. ☐

I would also like to receive further information on Pocket Classics. Please add me to your mailing list. ☐

Name ....

Address ....

....Postcode ....

Please return this form to: Regina Schinner, Sutton Publishing Ltd, Phoenix Mill, Far Thrupp, Stroud, Glos GL5 2BU.